COMBAT LEGEND

MESSERSCHMITT
Bf 109

Jerry Scutts

Airlife

Copyright © 2002 Airlife Publishing Ltd

First published in the UK in 2002
by Airlife Publishing Ltd

Text written by Jerry Scutts
Profile illustrations drawn by Dave Windle
Cover painting by Jim Brown – The Art of Aviation Co. Ltd

British Library Cataloguing-in-Publication Data
    A catalogue record for this book
    is available from the British Library

ISBN 1 84037 364 4

Printed in Hong Kong

For a complete list of all Airlife titles please contact:
Airlife Publishing Ltd
101 Longden Road, Shrewsbury, SY3 9EB, England
E-mail: sales@airlifebooks.com
Website: www.airlifebooks.com

Contents

Bf 109 Timeline

28 May 1935
First flight of Bf 109 V1 (WNr 758 D-IABI)

12 December 1935
First flight of Bf 109 V2 (WNr 759 D-IILU)

8 April 1936
First flight of Bf 109 V3 (WNr 760 D-IOQY)

23 September 1936
First flight of Bf 109 V4 (WNr 878 D-IALY)

5 November 1936
First flight of Bf 109 V5 (WNr 879 D-IIGO)

December 1936
Three pre-production aircraft sent to Spain for combat testing

11 November 1937
World Air Speed Record captured by Bf 109 V13 (WNr 1050 D-IPKY) at 379.51 mph (610.950 km/h)

18 December 1937
First flight of Bf 109 V15 (WNr 1773 D-IPHR/CE+BF) – first DB 601-powered aircraft

3/4 September 1939
Pilots of II./JG 77 shoot down a Wellington, the first RAF aircraft to fall to Bf 109s during WWII

22 November 1939
First captured Bf 109 evaluated by Allies (E-3 WNr 1304)

10 May 1940
27 *Gruppen* of Bf 109s spearhead German attack on France & the Low Countries

14 May 1940
The 'Day of the Fighters' over France – Bf 109s contribute significantly to the loss of 89 Allied aircraft

23 May 1940
First recorded victory by Bf 109E over a Spitfire (of No 92 Sqn RAF)

14 August 1940
First flight of Bf 109F-0 (converted Bf 109E WNr 2180/BY+BA)

30 September 1940
28 Bf 109s lost in action during the Battle of Britain – largest daily fighter loss to date

22 June 1941
20 *Gruppen* of Bf 109s spearhead German attack on Russia

8 September 1941
Bf 109Ts of JG 77 shoot down the first Boeing Fortress I lost by No 90 Sqn RAF

November 1941
Initial production of Bf 109G-1 (WNr 14001/YJ+WA and subsequent)

1 September 1942
Hans-Joachim Marseille of I/JG 27 shoots down 17 Allied aircraft over the Western Desert

5 November 1942
Erich Hartmann of JG 52 scores his first aerial victory over Russia

6 December 1942
First USAAF B-17 Fortress shot down by Bf 109Fs of JG 1

Feb-Mar 1943
Initial production of Bf 109G-6 (WNr 16313/BK+BC and subsequent)

July 1944
Initial production of Bf 109G-14/R-2 (WNr 163876 and subsequent)

September 1944
Initial production of Bf 109K-4 (WNr 330105 and subsequent)

November 1944
Initial production of Bf 109G-10 (WNr 130110 and subsequent)

1 January 1945
Nineteen Bf 109 *Gruppen* participate in the Operation *Bodenplatte,* the attack on Allied airfields in Holland & Belgium – 33 Bf 109s lost

7 April 1945
First and only large scale attempt by *Jagdwaffe* to bring down US bombers by ramming: 30-40 Bf 109s lost for eight bombers

8 May 1945
Erich Hartmann of JG 52 scores his 352nd and last aerial victory over Brunn, Germany

16 October 1948
Last known air combat between Bf 109 derivative Avia S 199 and Spitfires over Gaza, Egypt (one Royal Egyptian Air Force Spitfire shot down)

1. Messerschmitt Bf 109: Prototypes and Development

The reason behind the creation of the Messerschmitt Bf 109 was simple: when Germany created its new *Luftwaffe*, it had no world class fighter. In the mid 1930s it was clear that any new front line machine had to be of monoplane configuration, though a number of advanced features such as an enclosed cockpit, a retractable landing gear, variable pitch propeller, self-sealing fuel tanks and armour protection were also called for.

Destined to become an enduring classic among warplanes through its outstanding combat record, the Bf 109 met the criteria, enjoyed a massive production run of more than 30,000 examples and was a true cornerstone of the *Luftwaffe*. Had that air force lacked a fighter of such calibre it would have been sorely tested in battle, and very likely beaten at an early stage of the conflict.

As the world's air forces were beginning to realise in the mid-1930s, the monoplane was where the future of aviation lay. Despite such fighters having fought in World War I, a general adherence to the more traditional biplane had since prevailed. But in Germany the need to catch up with and if at all possible overtake the rest of Europe in regard to modern military aircraft forced through many advanced ideas. Hitler's National Socialist government supplied the will and the means to achieve that end.

On 1 March 1933, the charismatic Hermann Goering became head of the *Reichsluftfahrt-ministerium* (RLM, or Air Ministry). The ministry oversaw the clandestine development of a new air force that had been forbidden to

Germany under the terms of the Treaty of Versailles. State Secretary Erhard Milch headed the RLM, the most important department within which was the *Technische Amt*, directed, from 9 June 1936, by Oberst Ernst Udet. *Abteilung* LC II, a division within the technical office, was responsible for development of fighters and reconnaissance aircraft. In February 1934, the RLM issued development contracts for a monoplane fighter to BFW, Arado and Heinkel, and they tendered the Bf 109, the Ar 80 and the He 112 respectively. Focke-Wulf later submitted the Fw 159.

The 109's designer

The Bf 109 had emerged from the drawing board of Prof Willy Messerschmitt in 1935, the year that the *Luftwaffe* raised its first *Jagdgeschwader* equipped with Heinkel He 51 biplanes. Then technical director of Bayerische Flugzeugwerken at Augsburg, Messerschmitt had been a prodigious designer of sailplanes and light aircraft, and had latterly produced the Me 108. Featuring monocoque fuselage construction, stressed skin, a retractable undercarriage and leading edge slats, this four-seat liaison aircraft was a departure for Messerschmitt, who applied similar techniques to a new fighter for the *Luftwaffe*.

A cornerstone of Messerschmitt's design philosphy for the Bf 109 was simplicity and keeping overall size and weight to the very minimum; consequently the first example tipped the scales at only 3,970 lb (1 800 kg) in loaded condition. A low wing cantilever monoplane with a braced horizontal tailplane, the Bf 109 V1 incorporated wing slats to enhance low-altitude manoeuvrability. Aiming at ease of construction, Messerschmitt attached the main landing gear oleos to the fuselage rather than the wing, as was more usual. This enabled completed fuselages to be conveniently wheeled about during final assembly.

Following receipt of the development contract, Dipl.Ing Robert Lusser, BFW's project director, discussed the company's response at some length with staff engineer Robert Christensen. In his turn the RLM's Rolf W Lucht outlined the kind of design the ministry would favour. Confident that BFW could meet the requirement, the RLM asked for a tender.

A provisional mock-up was inspected at Augsburg on 11 May 1934. Discussion centred on the fighter's engine, which was then specified as the BMW 116. Armament was to be two fuselage-mounted MG 17 machine guns and a nose-mounted 20-mm MG/30L cannon located between the engine cylinders.

Confident about these details, Messerschmitt built an installation mock-up and Richard Bauer, head of the design bureau, prepared project and construction drawings. On 10 December 1934, the first metal was cut for the Bf 109 V1. Inspection of the design mock-up took place on 16 and 17 January 1935 and a report was subsequently prepared. On 25 April CII department head, Dr Ing Wolfram *Freiherr* von Richthofen, visited BFW and wrote a memo detailing his positive impressions of the prototype. BFW's engineers were not so confident; the BMW engine had been rejected in favour of the Junkers Jumo 210, but this was not yet available. With a first flight planned for May, BFW requested RLM assistance in finding a suitable engine and with the help of Ernst Heinkel, several Rolls-Royce Kestrel IIS engines rated at 583 hp were acquired.

First flight

With a powerplant installed and running, the Bf 109 V1 (WNr 758, civil-registered D-IABI) was readied for its maiden flight. It took off in the hands of Hans-Dietrich Knoetzsch on 28 May 1935 from the small airfield at Augsburg-Haunstetten. There were further test flights before the aircraft was flown to the experimental test centre at Rechlin on 15 October. In the meantime the inner wing skinning had had to be bulged over the wheel wells as the 'balloon' tyres fitted meant that the mainwheels could not fully retract.

Knoetzsch's comprehensive demonstration of the first Bf 109 included an aerobatic routine,

In the beginning – the first prototype, the Bf 109 V1, at Haunstetten airfield. Light and elegant, the first prototypes looked more like sporting than military aircraft, particularly with their two-bladed propellers driven by Rolls-Royce Kestrel engines. A technical data block appears on the rear fuselage. *(P Jarrett)*

Dr Helmut Wurster flying the Bf 109 V3 on 29 June 1936. This is one of a series of publicity photographs which were taken over the Lech River region, to the north of Augsburg. The barely discernible wording on the rear fuselage recorded part of the aircraft's basic technical specification. *(IWM)*

but disaster struck as he came into land. The aircraft bounced and slammed into the ground, sustaining substantial damage. It was ferried back to Augsburg. Early in 1936 Knoetzsch left Messerschmitt, to be replaced by Dr. Ing Hermann Wurster as the new BFW chief pilot. In the meantime, since Rechlin was then overburdened with development work, the repaired V1 had been evaluated at the naval test centre at Travemunde, which had spare capacity. The V 2 (WNr 759 /D-IILU) had also flown, on 12 December 1935.

Wurster collected D-IABI from Travemunde on 17 July 1936, after which it was used by the manufacturers for stall and spin tests and weapons installation trials. These flights lasted from August 1936 until January the following year, Wurster flying the prototype until 13 January when it was grounded and eventually scrapped. The demise of the Bf 109 V2, which crashed south of Travemunde after little more than three months, meant that the V3 (WNr 760/D-IOQY) which first flew on 8 April 1936, was the only Bf 109 then extant. The V3 became the prototype for the Bf 109A and was the first to carry armament. This was restricted to the two cowling machine guns, as the engine-

mounted cannon was proving troublesome. Testing the guns and items such as the R/T equipment became urgent, as examples of the Bf 109 were due to be delivered to *Jagdgruppe* 88 of the Condor Legion in Spain.

Testing in Spain

Powered by a 500 hp Jumo 210 C, the V3 went to Travemunde for testing on 1 July 1936, but the programme lagged. It included determining if the So-3 vertical bomb cell installed behind the pilot's seat would function correctly, as well as further engine and performance tests. The bomb cell idea was dropped after it was found that due to a lack of SC 10 electrical fuses the small bombs could only be released at low altitude. With the V4 having flown on 23 September, the V3 was crated up the following month and despatched by sea to Spain.

Having allowed for an engine-mounted cannon for the Bf 109 from the outset, further delays resulted in the Bf 109A dispensing with the means to use a weapon in this position pending remedial work.

An unknown number of Bf 109As were completed but at least 20 arrived in Spain, there being some indication that this logical

Factory fresh and with what may have been the last two digits of the Werke Nummer applied to the fuselage, an early Bf 109D is probably awaiting collection by a ferry pilot. The red stripe under the *Hakenkreuz* on the tail was a standard but short-lived application in early *Luftwaffe* service. *(Jarrett)*

designation was retrospectively applied to a series of pre-production aircraft that included several *Versuchs* examples.

The Bf 109 V4, which served as the prototype for the B series, also spent a brief period at Travemunde before it too was shipped to Spain on 30 November.

To make up for the lack of a cannon, the Bf 109B had a third MG 17 positioned to fire through the engine blast tube although this proved so troublesome in combat that it was removed from most machines operating in Spain. Reports that the two remaining machine guns were hardly lethal to enemy aircraft prompted Messerschmitt to design a new wing, incorporating two MG 17s or two 20-mm FF cannon. The so-called 'gun wing' was first tested on the Bf 109 V11 and V12.

Upon completion of the Bf 109A series, Augsburg began building the similar Bf 109B which was powered by the Jumo 210D. With the new single-seater and the Bf 110 sharing the assembly lines, the plant was soon at full capacity. Responsibility for the balance of the Bf 109B contract was therefore passed to Messerschmitt's Regensburg facility. In addition, the Fieseler Werke at Kassel and Erla Maschinenwerk in Leipzig were also licensed

by the RLM to build the aircraft. A total of 341 examples of the Bf 109B-1 were completed by these three companies.

High performance

Designed to be easy to mass produce, the Bf 109 was endowed with excellent performance by the standards of the late 1930s. It was powerful, manoeuvrable and fast, with a good rate of climb and an ability to reach an extreme height of 38,000 ft (11 582m). Most importantly, the new fighter's performance proved equal to if not better than the early foreign examples of a new generation of single seat interceptors then emerging: the Messerschmitt Bf 109 V1's first flight in 1935 preceeded that of the MS 406 and the Hurricane prototypes, both of which flew later that year, with the Spitfire and Fokker D XXI prototypes following in 1936. Of all the German fighter's potential adversaries, only the Polikarpov I-16 *Rata* was already in service when the Bf 109 first flew, the stubby Russian fighter having initially taken to the air in December 1933.

Production versions of all these new prototypes had their strong and weak points in terms of the necessary attributes. Ideally, a fighter needed speed, acceleration, and the ability to turn tightly in a dogfight. All these qualities the Bf 109 had in abundance, and reports of combat in Spanish skies revealed that the Bf 109 was an aircraft at the very pinnacle of modern aeronautical achievement. There was little to touch its all-round capability in the Iberian conflict, a fact that pilots of the Condor Legion eventually came to appreciate, although they were dubious at first.

Pilots unfamiliar with fast single seat monoplanes had to get used to the numerous advanced innovations that came with the new Messerschmitt. The Bf 109's high performance, its enclosed cockpit and radio telephone air-to-air-communications were among the features that had to be mastered.

The major drawback was the light armament fitted to the new fighter. The German machine's gunpower clearly lacked the punch required to destroy strong and well protected enemy aircraft, especially when compared to the cannon fitted to such types as the I-16 supplied by the Soviets to the Republicans.

At home BFW continued to produce Bf 109 development machines. The V11 flew on 1 March 1937 and was the first to test the gun wing, the two MG 17s being belt fed. Along with its twin fuselage guns the Bf 109's

ammunition load then totalled 3,000 rounds and the *E-Stelle* at Rechlin reported positive results from sustained firing trials.

Cannon experiments

For cannon firing tests the *E-Stelle* used the Bf 109 V12 (D-IVRU) and although these were generally satisfactory in terms of gun operation the wing clearly needed local strengthening to eliminate the skin wrinkling and rivet popping that occurred after prolonged firing. Until this work was carried out, the Bf 109's wing armament would be restricted to machine guns rather than cannon.

The Bf 109's fine showing at the 1937 Zurich flying competition focused much international attention on the potential of the aircraft and after Augsburg had completed 58 examples of the Bf 109C-1, the similar Bf 109D-1 was offered for export. Japan's initial interest in building the German fighter under licence was dropped in favour of the He 112, leaving Switzerland to become the first actual foreign customer, the *Flugwaffe* receiving the first of ten Bf 109D-1s in December 1938.

Chronologically the Bf 109 V13 and V14 can be considered as prototypes for the E series, as they were the first to be powered by the DB 601

A Bf 109B showing the prominent air intake atop the engine cowling, a feature that was also characteristic of the Bf 109D. The characteristic 'sit' of Jumo-engined Bf 109s is well shown in this view, as is the thin two-bladed propeller which did not exactly exude brute power. *(Jarrett)*

Fitting the Daimler Benz DB 601 powerplant totally altered the cowling contours of the Bf 109E compared to previous Jumo-engined models. This is an early 'Emil', on the strength of 2. *Staffel* of JG 20, which subsequently became 8./JG 51. The arched black cat badge was the official *Staffel* emblem.

but the true prototype was the V15, (D-IPHR). Physically larger than the Jumo and some fifty percent more powerful, the DB 601A drove a three bladed VDM airscrew; it also demanded a degree of cowling redesign to be shoehorned into the Bf 109's slender airframe.

In Germany the Bf 109E was the subject of tests to extend its range, one centring on a towing arrangement whereby the fighter would be hooked up to a transport aircraft. A programme aimed at overcoming the short range of the Bf 109 during cross Channel invasion operations, the glider tow link included a boss that fitted into the convenient orifice in the spinner intended for a centreline cannon. For years afterwards, this protrusion was taken to be the barrel of a cannon.

Production of the Bf 109E ran to about 4,000 aircraft, mainly in E-2, E-3 and E-4 versions, with a number of E-3s being tropicalised and others used as fighter-bombers designated E-4/B. The E-4/N designation was applied to those aircraft fitted with the 1,175 hp DB 601N, while the final E-7 was also a fighter bomber.

Regensburg built 144 Bf 109Es in 1939 with an additional 317 in 1940. This was not the complete output for 1940 as 11 Bf 109F-0s and 21 F-1s had been completed by December. All but the first two of the F series, which left the assembly shops in May 1940, were built in the last quarter as the Emil line was wound down. Bf 109E production ended in March 1941.

Carrier fighter

One of the more interesting test programmes associated with the Bf 109E, which for one reason or another did not come to fruition in the way they were planned, was the Bf 109T. This was a Bf 109E adaptation that anticipated Germany operating a seaborne fighter and dive bomber force built around the carrier *Graf Zeppelin*. Initial trials were conducted at Travemunde, where the Bf 109 V17 (WNr 1776/D-IYMS/TK+HK) was fitted with four catapult accelerator attachments and a tailhook, although this aircraft lacked the extended wings deemed necessary for carrier operation. Despite the fact that work on the *Graf Zeppelin* had already been suspended, the German carrier aircraft programme remained alive, and was not finally abandoned until 2 February 1943. In the meantime the extended wing was cleared for service and 70 Bf 109T conversions were made. These were subsequently de-navalised as far as deck-landing equipment was concerned, and they were issued to *Luftwaffe* units, principally JG 77, in 1941. As the extended wing Bf 109T-2, the 'Toni' gave long and useful service, mainly in far northern areas of the Reich.

One of the most unusual of the other programmes that led to actual service use was that of the *Beethoven Mistel* (Mistletoe). In this process, the fighter became the upper control component of a flying bomb adapted from the Junkers Ju 88 bomber. The first flight test utilising a Bf 109E and a DFS 230 glider took place on 21 June 1943. This and subsequent flights proved the practicality of separating the fighter from the lower component. Later combinations utilising a Bf 109F and Ju 88 were given the designation Mistel S 1.

As Germany's only modern fighter in the early war years a substantial number of Bf 109Es and Fs were used to test new equipment, including a ski undercarriage to improve operations from snow-covered airfields. Numerous aerodynamic improvements such as wing fences were also tried.

Alternative powerplants

Another more or less routine part of any experimental programme is to explore the feasibility of alternative engine installations as an insurance against the supply of the standard powerplant failing for one reason or other. Among the most extensive modifications of the Bf 109 was the grafting of an air-cooled radial in place of the liquid-cooled engine.

No example of the BMW 801, the preferred German engine, was available at the time Messerschmitt was ready to undertake flight testing, and once again the company turned to a foreign powerplant to get a Bf 109 prototype into the air. Accordingly it was a 1,200 hp Pratt & Whitney Twin Wasp with which the Bf 109 V21 (WNr 5602/CB+BN) took to the air on an unknown date between mid-1939 and September 1940. This engine provided useful data on handling characteristics and cooling properties, and the degree of re-engineering that would be necessary to adapt the Bf 109 to take a broader-chord cowling of a radial engine.

A BMW 801 was installed in the Bf 109X

Taking off for a sortie from Le Colombier, an airfield near JG 26's main base at Audembert, is Rolf Pingel, *Kommandeur* of I *Gruppe*. Pingel was a veteran of the Condor Legion, and in just three years had fought all over Europe. He had seen action over the United Kingdom, France, Belgium, Poland and Spain, and at the time this photo was taken had scored some 17 air-to-air victories. *(IWM)*

(D-ITXP) which made its maiden flight on 2 September 1940. The subsequent flying programme presumably gave adequate data but probably showed insufficient performance gain for Messerschmitt to seriously consider a change. Unfortunately, comprehensive figures on the Bf 109V21/Bf 109X engine test-bed trials do not appear to have survived. A further innovation, tested on the converted V21 and one that many pilots would have appreciated, was a 'bubble' canopy which offered much improved visibility.

A sleeker 'Friedrich'

The Bf 109 V21 later served as the prototype for the F series, the powerplant reverting to the DB 601. Two other aircraft, the V23 (WNr 5603) and V24 (WNr 5604) were involved in the test programme. These preceded the construction of at least 16 examples identified as Bf 109F-0 pre-production aircraft, WNr 5605–5620. These were built at Regensburg and there may have been an additional 11 examples (WNr 5621–5631) identified as Bf 109F-0s in company records although this remains unconfirmed. Subsequently both Regensburg and WNF built the F-1, although it enjoyed a modest production run of only 208 aircraft. Even fewer Bf 109F-2s were planned but by August 1941 1,380 had been completed.

Among the changes introduced during F series production was a remedy for the relatively high number of Bf 109s previously lost as a result of engine seizure. Liquid-cooled engines were notoriously prone to loss of coolant, and on the Bf 109 a minor puncture of the skin of one of the wing radiators was enough to cause an engine seizure within a matter of minutes. The Bf 109F-2 was the first to have radiator shut-off valves supplied as a field kit. These enabled either radiator to be shut down, thus conserving the coolant remaining in the system. Operation of the valves was often enough to allow a pilot to reach an airfield safely in an emergency.

Otherwise the F-2 initially retained some of the features of the Bf 109E including the triangular cockpit window at the base of the windscreen. Rounded wingtips replaced the squared-off tips of the Bf 109E and some F-2s had circular mainwheel wells. Drop tank provision was also standard on the majority of F-2s, the production of which was completed at Regensburg in September 1941, the plant having built 342 F-1s and F-2s that year.

Full details of the changes made to the 50 Bf 109F-3s are obscure but a revised radio fit is known, as is the fact that some were converted into two-seat trainers.

The next major production variant, the Bf 109F-4, followed the F-2 in service from June 1942 as far as operational units were concerned. Early examples were identical to the F-2 but as production proceeded the shape of the

Aesthetically the F model and the almost identical early model Gs had the cleanest lines of the entire Bf 109 series. These aircraft are F-2/trop (tropicalised) variants serving with I./JG 53. On their cowlings they display the *Pik-As* (Ace of Spades), long used by the *Geschwader* as its identification symbol.

Pictured on what was most probably a ferry flight, a Bf 109F-2 with *Stammkirchen* PK-HX formates with 'Black 1' presumably belonging to the unit which the new aircraft was en route to join. Apart from the reprofiled nose, the most obvious difference from the Emil is the lack of external tail bracing. (IWM)

supercharger air intake was revised and, unlike any examples of its predecessor, the F-4 was designed to have tropicalised air filtration equipment fitted on the production line to selected examples. Most aircraft had circular wheel wells and all were able to carry the standard external load consisting of either fuel tanks or bombs. Those examples fitted with GM-1 nitrous oxide injection boosters were known as the Bf 109F-4/Z and identified by an interim Fo 870 oil cooler under the nose.

To address the lightweight armament of the Bf 109F, WNF built 240 F-4/R1 versions which had provision for a pair of gondola-mounted MG 151/15 cannon. Known to have been used by JG 3 and JG 52, this installation remained a rarely fitted addition to a Bf 109F.

At least 43 Bf 109F-4s out of the 1,841 completed were built by Erla for the reconnaissance role. Different suffix numbers were used to denote the type of camera, which was carried as a single vertical installation behind the pilot's seat.

Although the Bf 109F series was to be extended into F-5, F-6 and F-8 versions, only a single F-5 was completed by WNF before production switched to the Bf 109G series. The major difference compared to the F series was the installation of the DB 605 engine which was to power all future versions.

In rounding out a brief development history of the Bf 109F, mention should be made of a further engine installation. This was the Jumo 213 with an annular radiator in similar configuration to that used to power the Ju 88 and the Fw 190 D series.

The 'Gustav'

Pending delivery of the DB 605 which would allow mass production of the Bf 109G to begin, Messerschmitt Regensburg installed a DB 601E in each of the first three examples (WNr 14001 to 14003). These Bf 109G-0s, completed at Regensburg (and actually identified in records as G-1s) during December 1941, were similar to the G-1 although the third aircraft of the trio (registered VJ+ WC), was modified to have a 'V' or butterfly tail assembly.

A one-off conversion, this new tail unit was evaluated in March 1943. Although only brief details have survived, the aircraft was apparently pleasant enough to fly, with

This Bf 109F of II./JG 27 serving in North Africa has a tropical filter over the supercharger air intake and a standard 66-gal (300 litre) drop tank. As the desert battles ranged over hundreds of miles, the short-ranged Bf 109 units sometimes had difficulty in offering the direct support they were there to provide.

characteristics not dissimilar to a standard Bf 109. The RLM decided against authorising any further conversions, however.

Similar in external appearance to the Bf 109F-4, the early Gustav incorporated the Fo 870 oil cooler and two small scoops on each side of the cowling to provide air to the exhausts and spark plugs. Other detail changes were made, and the propeller blade chord was slightly broader than before. The pressurised cockpit of the G-1 necessitated revision of the framing and the pilot's back armour, which had to be set vertically rather than angled forward as previously. It had welded instead of riveted cockpit framing, and the thickened frame incorporated a 60-mm armour glass panel in place of the separate panel that had been used previously. Small ventilation and air scoops

associated with pressurisation were also added. The G-1 also reverted to the squared off mainwheel wells as doors were to have been incorporated to improve airflow, although this was not done. Armament of the G-1 remained the same as before, the option of twin gondola mounted cannon being available but rarely taken up on front line aircraft.

Initially produced in parallel with the Bf 109G-1, the unpressurised G-2 was built at Erla and Regensburg. Production far outstripped the pressurised variant. WNF also switched to the new model, and by the time that the next variant was introduced, 1,587 Bf 109G-2s had been completed.

Field modifications

Among the *Rustsatze* applicable to the G-2 was

Although the Bf 109 was one of the earliest fighters to carry cannon armament, it lacked the firepower to deal with tough USAAF bomber targets over the Reich. A very necessary armament addition to the Bf 109G for bomber interception was two 20-mm gondola-mounted cannon, as seen on VD+VF. (Bundesarchiv)

the R1, which indicated an ETC 500 IX b bomb rack; the R2 which carried an ETC 50 VIId rack; and R6, the identifier for aircraft fitted with MG 151/20 external cannon. These supplementary designators were apparently not as widely used to qualify the aircraft role as is commonly believed, although several others were applicable to the G-2, the G-2 trop identifying the fitting of a large sand filter for the supercharger air intake.

Fifty pressurised Bf 109G-3s which were based on the G-1 but incorporated some G-4 features were built out of sequence. They were issued only to the high altitude *Staffeln* of JG 2, 11, 26 and 54.

The Bf 109G-4 was a direct descendant of the G-2. It was intended purely as a fighter and differed only in detail from earlier variants. It was built by the three main plants, plus Gyor Wagonfabrik of Hungary, and output ran to about 1,242 examples. The unpressurised G-4 weighed more than earlier models and to cope with this increased loading the mainwheel tyres were increased in size from 650 x 150-mm to 660 x 160-mm. A larger tailwheel tyre, of 350 x 135-mm was fitted in place of the 290 x 110-mm size used previously. The larger wheel would no longer fit the existing well, and the leg was

often locked down. Just to confuse things, some early production G-4s retained the smaller tyres while late production G-2s had the larger size. Larger mainwheels required a small fairing in the upper surface of each wing so that the well would completely enclose the retracted wheel.

Eighty Bf 109G-4/R3s were also built for the long-range reconnaissance role. These had hardpoints for two 66 Imp gal (300 litre) fuel tanks under the wings and provision for an Rb 75/30 or 50/30 camera; only the centreline cannon was retained, the cowling machine guns being removed. The gun troughs were sometimes faired over to reduce drag.

Bf 109 at its peak

When the Bf 109G-6 began reaching front line units in the Mediterranean in February 1943, Germany's leading fighter reached something of a design peak. This was the variant upon which all subsequent 109s were based, even though this was not the intention. In the event, more G-6s were built than any other sub-type, several thousand being completed up until 1945, enough to equip every fighter *Geschwader* in the *Luftwaffe* several times over.

A change in cowling gun armament to the MG 131 gave the G-6/R6 a long overdue boost

Drop tanks were good insurance if the short-legged Bf 109 had occasion to traverse open water. These Gustavs of JG 27 all carry the familiar centreline tank, but by early 1943 their only likely sea crossing was in the retreat from North Africa. However, new challenges were appearing over Germany itself, with Allied heavy bombers making their presence felt increasingly deep into the Reich. *(BA)*

in firepower compared to the light MG 17, but as there was insufficient internal space for the cartridge belt chutes used by the new guns, a characteristic rounded bulge was located aft on each side of the engine cowlings. The feature gave rise to the *Beule* or 'Bulge' nickname by which most late-war 109s were known. For real firepower, however, aircraft had to be fitted with underwing armament, the twin gondola cannon being supplemented by the alternative of twin rocket launching tubes for 210-mm air-to-air rockets from August 1943.

At about the same time the G-6 had the *Peilrufanlage* radio/navigational aid fitted, which required a D/F loop to be mounted on the fuselage spine. The radio mast was usually shortened but the 'long' mast was seen on some aircraft that had this equipment.

Increased pilot protection was afforded by the so called *Galland-Panzer*, which was a glass bullet-proof section cut into the head armour to improve rearward vision. Adolf Galland's name was also associated with a clear vision cockpit hood, more accurately identified as the *Erla-Haube* after its place of manufacture. Introduced in late 1943, the *Erla-Haube* was retrofitted to earlier aircraft, further confusing external identification. The same confusion

could arise when Bf 109G-6s began to receive a taller fin and rudder early in 1944 – this too could be fitted to early model Bf 109s. WNF built some G-6s for reconnaissance, the G-6/R2 and R3 respectively carrying Rb 50/30 and Rb 75/30 cameras. Other variants of the G-6 included aircraft equipped wth FuG 16Y radio for use by flight leaders to control other aircraft in combat, and those fitted with FuG 16ZE.

Even more power

By early 1944 the DB 605 engine had been successfully uprated by fitting a larger supercharger to become the DB 605 AS. Intended to improve the Bf 109's high altitude performance, the DB 605 AS required a redesign of the engine cowling to incorporate the supercharger and new engine bearers. At the same time the MG 131 machine gun feed fairings were recontoured and this new cowling, along with an enlarged supercharger air intake, significantly altered the aircraft's profile. The taller fin and rudder were invariably fitted to the G-6/AS to counteract the greater engine torque and to conserve aluminium as Germany's raw material situation worsened, several sections of this unit were constructed from wood.

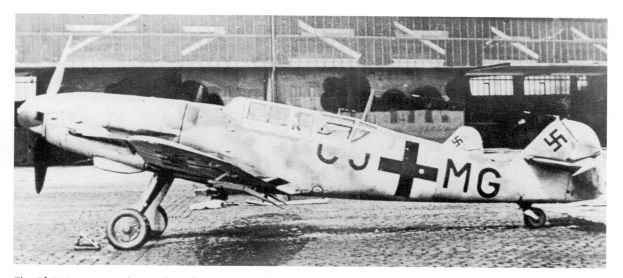

The Bf 109 was a tricky machine for novices to fly, so the Bf 109G-12 two-seat trainer was much appreciated by harassed *Luftwaffe* flying instructors when it first appeared early in 1944, much later than they might have wished. All 500 aircraft which entered service were converted from existing airframes, the aircraft shown having being built as a G-6/trop, as the two umbrella holders indicate.

The majority of the Bf 109G-6/AS variants, totalling 686 aircraft, were converted from existing airframes. Only 226 were built as new by sub-contractors that included Blohm und Voss. Deliveries began in the late spring of 1944 with *Gruppen* of JG 1, JG 5 and JG 11 being the first recipients and NJGr 10, JG 3 and JG 27 following suit soon afterwards. By that time production of the G-5, the last pressurised Bf 109 variant, was virtually complete. In essence the G-5 resembled an early G-6 in that it reverted to the framed canopy with vertical head armour and with silicagel pellets inserted in the canopy glazing. The G-5 could carry the range of *Rustsatze* applicable to the standard fighter unless the DB 605AS engine was fitted, in which case, pressurisation was dropped – as it was on all subsequent variants.

Photo Reconnaissance

The Bf 109G-8 was designed to provide tactical reconnaissance units with something more capable to fight with. It became the standard fighter for such *Gruppen* until the end of the war. Deliveries commenced in November 1943.

Also similar to the Bf 109G-6, the G-8 had additional camera provision, being capable of accommodating two vertically-mounted Rb 12.5/7 x 9 cameras or a single Rb 32/7 x 9. Both the original and taller vertical tail surfaces were fitted and G-8s were also flown with either of the two styles of cockpit canopy.

The belated attempt to incorporate all the improvements introduced on the Bf 109G-6, the G-14 was another model that appeared out of strict numerical sequence. In terms of the stated aim of standardisation the aircraft was a complete failure, as it appeared in as many different guises as the G-6. Production began in July 1944 (WNr 163876, a G-14/R-2 is believed to have been the first example) and probably extended to 5,500 or more. Although it was far from standardised in terms of equipment, the G-14 replaced the G-6 as the baseline Bf 109 for the remainer of the war, all first line and many second line units receiving it.

Early model G-14s were powered by the DB 605A and had the early-type tail unit although the *Erla-Haube* was standard. Otherwise a G-14/AS was indistinguishable from the G-6/AS which it replaced, some aircraft even being fitted with the shallower Fo 870 oil cooler, though this was considered inadequate compared to the deeper Fo 987 type. By mid-1944, however, there was a positive move towards building only the Bf 109G-14 (mostly

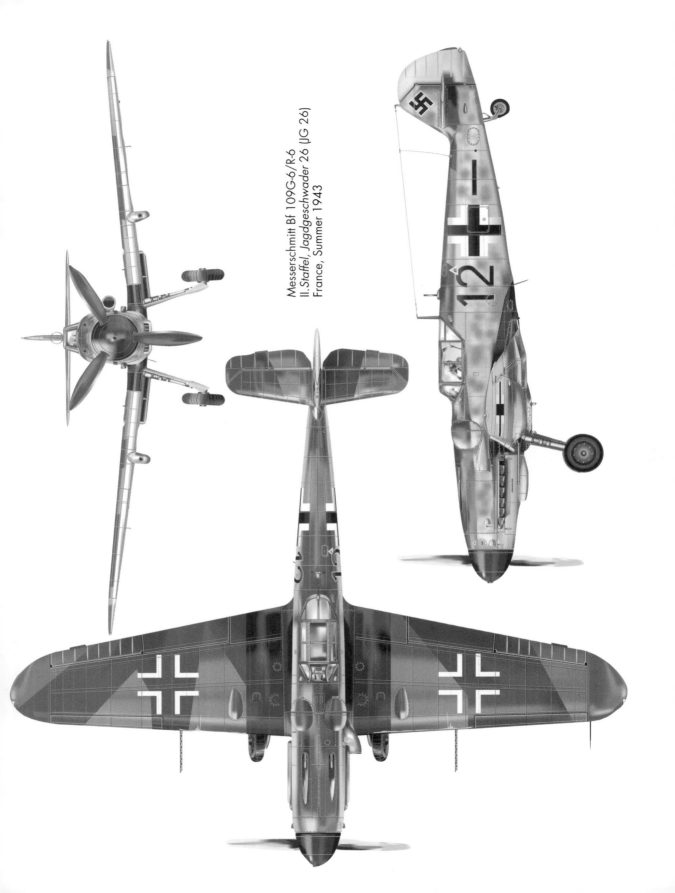

Messerschmitt Bf 109G-6/R-6
II.*Staffel, Jagdgeschwader* 26 (JG 26)
France, Summer 1943

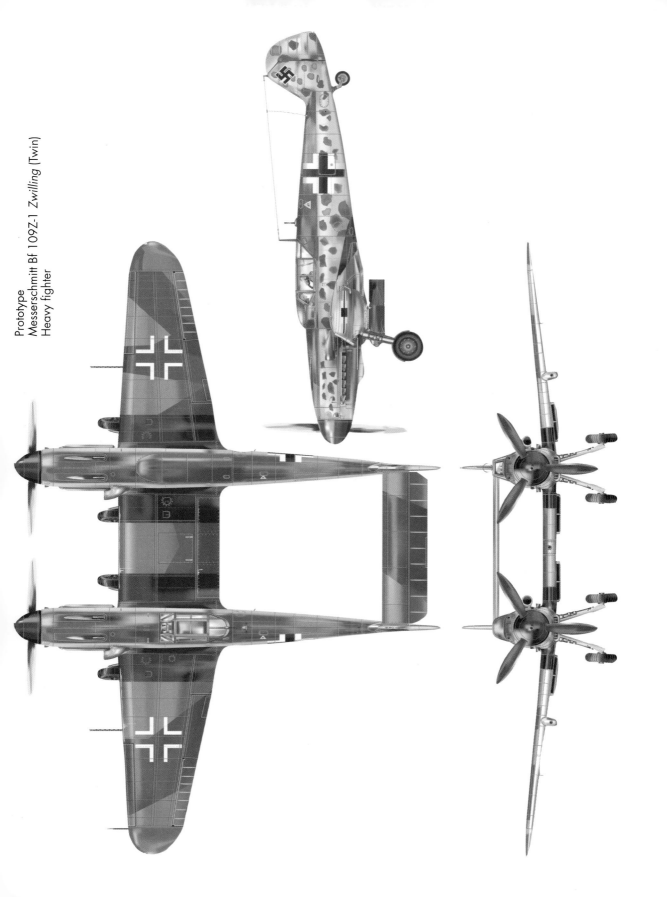

Prototype
Messerschmitt Bf 109Z-1 *Zwilling* (Twin)
Heavy fighter

One of the most ingenious uses of the Bf 109 was as a control aircraft for the Bf 109/Ju 88A *Mistel* combination, seen above and below on an early proving flight. Bf 109F-4 (CI+MX) was the first fighter used in the tests to show that 'Project Beethoven' was a practical possibility. At the moment of release the Bf 109F lifted smoothly away and the explosive packed Ju 88 headed for its target. At least, that was the intention, but the war situation had deteriorated too far for the *Mistels* to be used in action with much hope of success. *(E J Creek)*

in G-14/AS form), the last known G-6 having been completed at Regensburg in July as part of a mixed batch which included G-14s. The five examples in question had WNr 782340 to 782344, although all these would have logically been identified as G-14s.

Bf 109K-4

As near a standardised variant as the later Bf 109s ever got, the K-4 generally incorporated the improvements made on the late production Bf 109G, including the taller vertical tail surfaces, larger mainwheel tyres and distinctive re-contoured engine cowlings necessary to enclose the DB 605D. However, some early aircraft were powered by the DB 605AS engine.

Regensburg began building the Bf 109K-4 in September 1944, but detail differences belied the standardisation goal; long and short tailwheel legs, different location points for the FuG radio aerial and fittings for mainwheel doors were just some of the contrasts to be observed on operational airfields.

As was usual, front line units made their own changes which were usually aimed at weight saving and thereby increasing performance and/or manoeuvrability. Few

pilots would think twice about taking off without a set of undercarriage doors though the saved weight was offset by increased drag.

All Bf 109K-4s had *Werke Nummeren* in the 330000 to 571000 range. Actual deliveries to *Luftwaffe* units are believed to have run to about 1,600 examples.

2. Operational History: 109s in Combat

Any aircraft designed for combat will only really be proven when it is actually flown under battlefield conditions. To test the Bf 109, some prototypes and early production aircraft were shipped to Spain to assist Franco's Nationalist cause. Taken on strength by *Jagdgruppe* 88 of the Condor Legion at Tablada, the Bf 109 V3, V4, V5 and V6 were joined by the first examples of 69 B series aircraft. Five Bf 109Cs and 36 Bf 109Ds followed. It proved to be a fortuitous move by the Germans.

During the course of his operational sorties over Spain, Werner Mölders refined several fluid, highly flexible fighter formations that had been in vogue late in WWI. Built around the 'finger four' – aircraft spaced like the finger tips of an outstretched hand – this formation was based on two pairs, or *rotte*, each consisting of a leader and wingman; it allowed each pilot the maximum freedom of movement and visibility while covering each others' blind spots. When the Legion returned after the war ended on 30 March 1939, pilots who had flown the Bf 109 had gained months of vital combat experience.

In Germany the first Bf 109s to join an operational unit were the D models issued to JG 132 at Doberitz. On 12 March 1938 a *Staffel* of Bf 109Ds of I./JG 135 flew into Wien-Aspern to support the Austrian *Anschluss*, detaching a *Kette* of three aircraft to Linz. Apart from providing the *Luftwaffe* with a valuable pool of Austrian airmen, the annexation also provided an excellent base for future production of the Bf 109, at Wiener Neustadt.

Deliveries of Bf 109s proceeded slowly in 1938, bringing about an average inventory of 26 aircraft per *Gruppe*. When the Czech crisis also passed peacefully, the *Luftwaffe* continued to train, modernise and prepare for battle. Mindful of the British pledge to go to war in the event that Poland was attacked, the *Luftwaffe* leadership kept the most modern fighters in Germany. A deficit in production of Bf 110s led to ten twin-engine *Zerstörergruppen* being equipped with Bf 109s and given temporary *Jagdgruppe* designations.

Action over Poland

By the time of the invasion of Poland on 1 September 1939, eleven *Gruppen* had converted to the Bf 109E. Thirteen were still equipped with the Bf 109D, while two were in the process of converting from the Dora to the Emil. Several units participated in the 18-day campaign to subdue Poland – *Luftflottenkommandos* 1 and 4 controlled twelve and four *Gruppen* of Bf 109s respectively – but the bulk of the fighters remained in Germany on home defence.

When the Western Allies made no military moves against Germany, the *Luftwaffe* had time to make good the operational losses it had suffered in Poland, and used the time to continue to modernise its fighter force. During the first few months of World War II the *Jagdwaffe's* interceptors remained a mixture of Bf 109Ds and Es, but by the spring of 1940 the latter sub-type had all but replaced the Jumo-engined model, which was then transferred to a useful training role.

A Bf 109B named 'Luchs' stands under the Spanish sun in readiness for another sortie with *Jagdgruppe* 88 of the Condor Legion. Pleased as they were to be given one of the world's most modern fighters, *Luftwaffe* pilots flying in Spain were nevertheless critical of the Bf 109's lack of firepower. *(Jarrett)*

Skirmishes on the Franco-German border resulted in losses of fighters and reconnaissance aircraft as both sides attempted to gain a picture of the other's operational readiness. Bf 109s clashed with French and RAF fighters before the severe winter of 1939/40 drastically curtailed air operations on the Western Front. Such periods of enforced idleness were put to good use by the *Luftwaffe*, which continued to establish new *Gruppen* and to increase the number of Bf 109Es in service.

The massive 10 May attack on France and the Low Countries included nearly the total striking power of the *Luftwaffe*. Almost the entire fighter force was committed: only two complete *Gruppen* plus two *Staffeln* remained to defend Germany. The front line commanders could thus call upon 14 *Gruppen* with 613 Bf 109Es in *Luftflottenkommando* 2, and 13 *Gruppen* with 601 fighters in *Luftkdo* 3, a total unit establishment of 1,214 fighters. Flying units

Hans Schmoller-Haldy in front of his personal Bf 109B in Spain. Note the casual 'local' nature of his uniform, a product of the lengths the Germans went to in order to disguise their involvement in the conflict. *(Schmoller-Haldy)*

With the Bf 109E replacing the earlier Jumo-engined models the *Luftwaffe* mounted numerous exercises to simulate war conditions. These aircraft were part of I./JG 20 (later 7./JG 51) during such an exercise.

rarely enjoy 100 per cent serviceability, so the actual deployable *Jagdwaffe* strength on the 10th was 874 Bf 109Es, a figure that obviously fluctuated as a result of combat attrition.

That these numbers were more than sufficient was obvious from the start. France fielded many MS 406 fighters but few of the more modern Dewoitine D520s which were closer to a match for the Bf 109.

The *Armée de l'Air* found it difficult to adequately support French ground forces, and neither could a fragmented air defence be regenerated by British Expeditonary Force Hurricane squadrons. The *Jagdflieger* shrugged off their own losses and on 14 May intensive air action unfolded as the German breakthrough at Sedan was contested by Allied bomber attacks on the bridges over the Albert Canal. The result was carnage on an unprecedented scale as the *Jagdflieger* went to work. By the evening, 89 Allied aircraft had been destroyed – to the Germans the 14th was the 'Day of the Fighters'.

In combat the Bf 109 generally did well against the French fighters it encountered although few large scale air battles actually materialised. Bf 109 formations rarely met Hurricanes in direct confrontation, however, but when they did honours were often about even. The Hurricane was an excellent gun platform and could out-turn the Bf 109 at low altitude but the German machine could always outclimb and outdive its opponent. Superior battle tactics often turned an engagement to the Germans' advantage.

Further suicidal assaults on key ground targets by French and British bombers could not check the German Panzer spearheads, which were on the Channel coast by early June. Patrolling out over the Channel as the British Army evacuated Dunkirk, the Bf 109s began meeting a British fighter that seemed as good as their hard-working Emils. Even so, few of them were worried, despite the fact that they had no idea how many Spitfires the RAF possessed.

Battle over Britain

To bring about conditions for an invasion of Britain, Germany had to neutralise Royal Air Force Fighter Command. The *Luftwaffe* mustered sixteen *Gruppen* of Bf 109Es under *Jagdfliegerfuhrer* 2, with 513 operational aircraft out of an establishment of 590. Nine *Gruppen* were assigned to *Luftflottenkommando* 3, with 334 operational machines out of 386. These 25 *Gruppen* would fly *Freie Jagd* (free hunting) sorties and escort the dive and medium bomber force, much as they had before. Careful tactical planning to beat a new, well organised foe seemed unimportant to men flying the aircraft that was the master of Europe's skies.

The *Kanalkampf* ('Channel Battle', the name used by the Germans for the key stages of the Battle of Britain) began in July 1940, with a series of probes against Britain's coastal shipping and port defences. The *Jagdwaffe* continued to increase its strength, materially if not numerically, with the latest model Bf 109Es. Escorting bombers by maintaining a watchful top cover the German fighters achieved some localised sucess but from the beginning it was

A ground crewman adds the thirty-second bar to the rudder of Werner Mölders' Bf 109E (WNr 2804). By 28 August 1940 the brilliant 'Vati' had scored his twenty-eighth kill, with four more being added to his tally by the 31st, the date of this photograph. *(IWM)*

clear how the pattern of battle was shaping. Larger and larger bomber formations made the *Jagdfliegers'* task of protecting their twin-engined charges extremely difficult. Their free-ranging patrols could knock down the enemy – but in many instances the RAF refused to dogfight the dangerous formations of Messerschmitts and saved their ammunition for the real target – the bombers.

Close bomber escort

Fighter operations were seen as secondary by the Germans, as the Bf 109E lacked the endurance to fly far inland to attack Fighter Command on the ground. Ordering ever closer bomber escorts, Hermann Goering removed freedom of action from his deadly fighters. Few drop tanks were available for the *Jagdwaffe* to increase the meagre range of the Bf 109s, and the prospect of another 'easy' victory became more and more remote.

As the summer of 1940 wore on, German fighter pilots grew to detest the waters of the Channel which proved too wide for many damaged aircraft and wounded pilots. By the time the Bf 109F-1 entered operational service with JG 51 in October, the number of daylight sorties against England had been greatly reduced. The *Jagdwaffe* was largely pulled back from France to re-equip – and to absorb replacements for those pilots who had been lost flying the 600 Bf 109Es that did not return.

Although some highly skilled pilots such as Werner Mölders, *Kommodore* of JG 51, were delighted with the enhanced manoeuvrability of the *Friedrich*, others, notably Adolf Galland of JG 26, had reservations. He was convinced that the lighter armament of the new model Bf 109 was a retrograde step.

The gradual expansion of a cross Channel offensive by RAF Fighter Command in 1941 now saw the *Luftwaffe* fighting on terms more favourable to itself. As the short range limitations of the Spitfire V and Hurricane II were similar to their own Bf 109Es operating over the Channel the previous year, the *Jagdwaffe* could afford to bide its time.

Portents of events to come were revealed in a small way on 8 September, when the fighter controller in Norway alerted a *Rotte* of Bf 109Ts of I./JG 77 to intercept unidentified bombers at high altitude. Climbing to 25,000 ft (7 629m) the Messerschmitts found four Boeing Fortress Is of No 90 Squadron, RAF and in a running fight, downed three of them. Daylight incursions by enemy heavy bombers were something of a rarity since the RAF had switched mainly to night attacks – largely as a result of Bf 109s and -110s making short work of Wellingtons operating against German capital ships in 1939.

Bf 109s were gradually removed from the *Zerstörergruppen* once the Bf 110 force was expanded. The Messerschmitt single seater had also been used in early night defence experiments, cooperating with searchlights and flak units pending the arrival of dedicated night fighters.

The RAF continued to mount occasional raids by day, and from 1942 the British began using improved American-built medium bombers against European targets. Some were intercepted, but there was little effort made by the *Luftwaffe* to mount a positive campaign against the raiders.

North Africa

In the meantime Mussolini's expansionist plans for the Middle East had foundered on British resistance. Hitler sent aid to his fellow fascist dictator, in the form of *Fliegerkorps* X and the

Bf 109E pilots of *Stab./JG 53* with a friendly dog which may have done duty as the *Staffel* mascot. A very common sight around the *Jagdwaffe's* aerodromes, as well as on those of their opponents across the channel, interest in such pets helped ease the strains of operational flying. *(IWM)*

One of the 600 Bf 109s the *Luftwaffe* lost on the Channel front in 1940 was this E-1 (WNr 6296) flown by *Oberleutnant* Werner Bartels, Technical Officer of *Stab./*III JG 26. It crashed on 24 July near the Margate-Broadstairs railway line and was displayed in Fairfield car park in Croydon, Surrey. *(IWM)*

Afrika Korps. Bf 109Es were first despatched in February 1941, and over North Africa the pilots found a theatre of war well suited to their proven and flexible *Freie Jagd* tactics. Up against a large but often ill-coordinated variety of Allied aircraft, the desert *Jagdflieger* performed well although they were always spread thin, especially when called upon to escort the slow Junkers Ju 87 Stuka.

His sights now set firmly on Russia, Hitler launched a curtain-raising campaign to secure his flank in the Balkans beginning on 6 April 1941. In another lightning victory for German arms, Yugoslavia fell, her air forces subjected to a *Blitzkrieg* which saw German Bf 109Es briefly pitted against similar fighters previously sold to the Yugoslav Air Force.

JG 27 *Afrika* retained its Emils for months, only being re-equipped with the Friedrich in late 1942 when the unit was joined by JG 53 *Pik-As*. Further reinforcements included Joachim Muncheberg's 7./JG 26, whose brief, highly successful deployment over and around Malta in the spring of 1941 demonstrated how effective well-flown Bf 109Es could still be.

That fact was rammed home forcefully when LG 2 and JG 77 sought out Royal Navy ships

covering the British evacuation of Crete after the island had been taken by the Germans. In cooperation with Ju 87s these Messerschmitt *Jabos* sank and damaged several British warships which could ill be spared at that time.

Invasion of Russia

The *Luftwaffe's* greatest campaign began in the early hours of 22 June 1941. Operation *Barbarossa*, the German invasion of the USSR, could call on the strength of three *Luftflotten* or Air Fleets. Each was assigned to support one of the *Wehrmacht's* three army groups, attacking through the northern, central and southern sectors of the massive front. *Luftflotte* 1, supporting Army Group North, had four *Gruppen* of Bf 109s. *Luftflotte* 2 was assigned to Army Group Centre which was directed at Moscow and had nine Bf 109 *Gruppen* on strength. *Luftflotte* 4 with seven *Gruppen* was assigned to Army Group South, driving through the Ukraine.

Most fighter *Geschwadern* were equipped with the Bf 109F, only II./JG 54 and II. and III./JG 27 retaining Bf 109Es, primarily as fighter bombers. JG 77 was in the process of exchanging its Emils for the Bf 109F, but only its

The Bf 109E saw a great deal of service in the Western Desert in the early days of the German intervention in the region. Here, pith-helmeted ground crew put some final touches to an E-4/trop of JG 27, which has the air intake filter masked to prevent fine sand from getting into the engine. *(BA)*

III./*Gruppe* had begun the process. At the start of the campaign there were 619 serviceable Bf 109s out of an establishment total of 793.

During the opening weeks of the assault on the Soviet Union, the *Luftwaffe* exploited another weak air defence, hamstrung by vast distances and poor lines of communication. The surprise attack enabled bombers and fighters to destroy much of the Red Air Force on the ground, the Bf 109Es using, among more conventional weapons, dispensers of SD-2 anti-personnel bomblets which proved particularly deadly against airfields, lethal to both personnel and aircraft.

Using one forward airfield after another, even the fighter *Gruppen* had difficulty keeping up with the racing Panzers; supplied almost entirely by air, the Bf 109s put down on barren strips of steppe, refuelled, rearmed and took off repeatedly to sweep the skies of enemy bombers, many of which were sacrificed in suicidal, uncordinated attempts to stem the German advance. Inexperienced Soviet bomber crews died in their hundreds as the *Jagdflieger* wrought terrible destruction on their formations.

By the autumn the army spearheads were poised to secure their main obectives, the cities of Moscow and Leningrad. But the change in seasons set in to foil these plans. With the arrival of 'General Winter', the *Luftwaffe* fighter force became a 'fire brigade', shuttling from sector to sector to cover the stalled ground forces whenever Russian armies (which enjoyed organic air cover) counter-attacked. The Bf 109 remained the cornerstone of the

When the Germans turned East the Bf 109E was fast being replaced by the F series, but numbers were still in service. This camouflaged Emil was part of JG 52 prior to the air assault on the Balkans in the spring of 1941.

Luftwaffe fighter arm, even though it had been joined in the front line in 1942 by the new, and in many ways superior Focke-Wulf Fw 190. This was partly because the almost inevitable teething troubles inherent in any new design curtailed the 190's early effectiveness.

Several examples of the new Bf 109G-0 entered service with JG 2's 11./*Staffel* in June 1942. Established as a special high altitude formation, this unit was joined in August by 11./JG 26 with a similar mission. The Bf 109G-1 also entered service with JG 1, JG 51 and JG 53 and with JG 77 in Norway.

The 1942 summer offensive in Russia was aimed at the oilfields in the Caucasus. To protect the *Wehrmacht's* northern flank, it was decided that Stalingrad needed to be taken – a fateful decision. Heavily committed to reducing the city, the *Luftwaffe* faced an increasingly strong Red Air Force. Still able to maintain local air superiority, the *Jagdflieger* notched up a steadily rising tally of kills – but as more and more Soviet strength was fed into the battle zone their efforts gradually began to resemble trying to hold back the tide.

By the beginning of 1943, the German Sixth Army was trapped in the city, and in spite of tremendous efforts on land and in the air it was destroyed. The fierce fighting proved immensely costly to the *Luftwaffe*, which lost many of its most able fighter pilots. But even though the ranks of the pre-war trained men had been thinned and replaced by men who had not enjoyed the same lengthy nurturing for combat, the replacements generally fought

well, inspired by the surviving *Experten*, the 'old hares' who invariably led from the front, often from the cockpit of a Bf 109.

Defeat in Africa

A similar pattern of initial success followed by a gradual relinquishing of the initiative to superior forces took place in North Africa. Having failed to subdue Malta, Operation Torch and the battle of El Alamein had forced the Axis forces in the desert onto the defensive. Outnumbered in the air, bombed on its airfields and forced to abandon precious aircraft, the *Jagdwaffe* soon lost any further chance to influence events. By September 1942 the Bf 109 units could muster but 80 fighters, with an estimated 800 Allied fighters opposing them.

The loss of Tunisia, Sardinia and Sicily was followed by the surrender of Italy in September 1943. Ordered up against the heavy bombers of the new 15th Air Force, the *Jagdflieger* suffered heavily. When the Allies marched into Rome on 5 June 1944 the southern front had become a bitterly fought sideshow for German air operations, yet JG 77 and other fighter units soldiered on for a few more months.

In the West, 17 August 1942 was a date not noted as particularly significant by the *Jagdwaffe*. For some weeks the initial incursions into continental Europe by B-17 Flying Fortresses of the US 8th Air Force were not recognised as the highly dangerous pointers to the future that they actually were. The defence of the bombers' targets, as yet only in occupied Europe, was often left to the *Luftwaffe*'s capable

When the winter snow struck in Russia, man emulated nature and applied a white coat to many front line aircraft. This Bf 109F of JG 54 carries a typical example of the kind of winter camouflage used.

flak units. Not until December did JG 1 claim the first of the four-engined heavies to fall to the Bf 109F.

Defence of the Reich

When they finally did appreciate the threat that a sustained American precision bombing campaign posed for their most vital war production plants in the Reich, the Germans reacted strongly. Judging the heavies, rather than any amount of mediums, to be their prime target, the *Luftwaffe* high command deployed the Bf 109 in conjunction with the Fw 190, twin-engined fighters and flak batteries to bring down as many of them as possible. By waiting until any short-range Allied escort fighters (Spitfires and P-47 Thunderbolts) had had to

turn for home, the *Jagdflieger* could pounce on the bombers with far less risk. Once pilots had experienced what they were up against, the true magnitude of this task became clear. The big *viermots* (four motors, slang term for heavy bombers) were tough nuts to crack, and Reich defence soon gained a reputation as the toughest war theatre of them all.

The US bomber formations presented an awesome series of targets. Each formation typically occupied an area of sky some 850 feet (260 m) deep and several miles long, the bomber boxes being staggered and stacked up in elements to uncover the maximum number of defensive guns, up to 12 per aircraft.

Head-on attacks were widely employed by the *Jagdwaffe* during 1943. Typically, Bf 109s or

Fw 190s would formate with a selected box of bombers, out of defensive gun range. They then curved around ahead of the bombers and to make their firing runs, closed variously to between 800 and 300 yards (730-275 m) before breaking away. Some pilots specialised in boring in to within 100 yards (91 m) of the big bombers to maximise their chances of making a kill. By varying their individual runs, the German pilots aimed to confuse the gunners and present them with multiple targets. Adopting this and other interception tactics including the high speed dive and breakaway known as the 'roller coaster' and the 'scissors' in which pairs dived on the target from two directions simultaneously, the Germans took a steady toll of the American attackers.

Galland's encouragement

General der Jagdflieger Adolf Galland was an enthusiastic proponent of the head-on attack. Having personally demonstrated that a Bf 109 could make such a pass and survive even a 'flat' exit through the top turret fire of the bombers, he urged the *Jagdwaffe* to adopt this and other methods that lessened the risk to pilots. The leading B-17s remained primary targets because the Germans soon realised that the loss of highly experienced lead crews, which usually included group bombardiers and navigators, might result in a below-standard bomb pattern, thus minimising the degree of destruction at the target.

Although 1943 is recalled as the year in which the unescorted US heavies were martyred, German pilot casualties also increased steadily. Few assaults on the bomber formations were completed entirely without fighter losses. Although high speed breakaways were favoured, the sheer momentum of many attacks often took the fighters right through the formations, the pilots having little choice but to plunge through and risk the vicious crossfire from the B-17 and B-24 gunners.

A watershed in the European air offensive occurred on 17 August when the Americans bombed Schweinfurt and Regensburg. Only well into the mission did the German ground controllers realise that the Messerschmitt factory was one of the targets, whereupon the Bf 109s and their companions in the Fw 190

Gruppen exacted a terrible toll of the bombers. Even with the loss of 60 B-17s, the Americans returned to the same targets in October, only to lose the same number again. However, the magnitude of this disaster did not force the Americans to discontinue the offensive – instead, they increased efforts to deploy long range fighters for 'all the way' bomber escort.

With additional wing cannon enabling the Bf 109G to be a more effective bomber destroyer, a further boost to the aircraft's firepower was provided by a pair of WGr 121 rocket launchers. First used during the initial Schweinfurt-Regensburg mission, these weapons were not universally adopted, units usually grouping their rocket-capable Bf 109Gs into a single *Staffel*. As the rockets were technically field modifications fitted at unit rather than factory level, this policy centralised the small degree of specialist training required for the ground crews to install them. For their part, the pilots could work together to determine tactical deployment for maximum effect and conduct useful post-mission critiques of the results obtained in combat.

Since spring 1943 US bombers had been escorted by P-47s, with longer ranged P-38 Lightnings appearing that autumn. These fighters were increasingly dangerous foes for the German defenders. But neither Thunderbolts nor Lightnings were as yet flying very deeply into Germany, and the *Jagdwaffe* avoided them for as long as possible. Heavy bombers were and would remain their prime target.

At their substantial operating altitudes the American Fortresses and Liberators now came up against Bf 109Gs which could fly and fight well in the thin air at 25,000 to 35,000 ft (7 650– 10 660 m). Repeated incursions over the German heartland brought about bitter air battles in which the defending fighters inflicted a spiralling number of American casualties.

Taking on the escorts

A broad system evolved whereby the Bf 109s would undertake to deal with any escort fighters while the Focke-Wulfs with their heavier calibre cannon armament and armour could deal with the bombers. In reality things did not always go according to such a tidy plan, and the '190s often mixed it up with the

American bombers flew in densely-packed boxes, the close formation enabling up to 50 bombers at a time to engage incoming fighters. On anything but a head-on pass, a Bf 109 attacking the formation might be faced with the concentrated fire of as many as 200 out of the 600 heavy machine guns carried by aircraft like these B-17s of the 91st Bomb Group, 8th Air Force. (USAF)

escort. Even so, the Bf 109 with its better performance at height remained the *Luftwaffe*'s premier high altitude interceptor.

A problem the massed interceptors always faced was that unless maximum damage was caused to the target bombers in the initial firing passes, repeating the process in similar strength became almost impossible. After firing, the German pilots made a high speed break away to avoid defensive fire and became widely scattered across miles of sky. There was often no time to reform for repeat assaults before the bombers passed through a given defence sector, by which time the fighters had to land and refuel. Other *Gruppen* would then take their place as the bombers passed into other defensive sectors.

In mid-1943, with the Bf 109G-6 only just

holding its own against a number of excellent Allied designs, Messerschmitt attempted to rationalise the improvements made to the *Luftwaffe*'s standard interceptor. It was a programme that largely failed in its purpose, principally because the scope for modification was lessened if there was the slightest risk of disrupting production and reducing the flow of fighters to the front line units.

By December 1943 the Messerschmitt and Focke-Wulf pilots found themselves pitted against a new American escort fighter of superior performance. The North American P-51B Mustang also possessed the range to accompany the bombers right into Germany.

For the *Jagdwaffe*, successive new sub variants of the Bf 109 showed little improvement on the last; while it was effective

While the bulk of the *Luftwaffe's* fighter strength was sucked into the fight over the Reich, a small force had to remain on the Channel coast for interception duty against the RAF's fighter and bomber operations. The red cockerel cowling badge on this Bf 109F indicates that it belongs to III./JG 2, which was one of these units. *(BA)*

against the heavies the high-drag *Kannonboot* Gustav suffered a performance loss that could verge on the suicidal in combat with Mustangs. More heavily armed and armoured Fw 190s faced much the same problem.

In 1944, Gunther Rall was chased by the Bf 109's other deadly American fighter adversary, the P-47 Thunderbolt.

"We went 'tally ho' against a group of P-47s, Zemke's Wolfpack. His first element pulled over but the second element chased me down to treetop level. When I crash landed, I had been hit and the Bf 109 was all shot out."

It was the second injury Rall had suffered during his combat career. He was hospitalised to recover from his wounds, an enforced break that probably saved his life. He ended the war with 275 kills, the majority gained on the 109.

By D-Day the *Luftwaffe* fighter force in the West was a shadow of its former strength.

Despite rushing elements of most Bf 109 *Gruppen* to France, the German high command could do little to hamper the juggernaut that was the Allied tactical air forces. Having to distribute their forces to Northern France, the Reich and the East brought about a massive logistical problem.

109s in the Night

Despite having been used in the development of the *Himmelbett* night defensive system, the Bf 109 carried no specialised night-fighting equipment before the advent of the G-6. In order to provide the pilot with more positive means of detecting enemy aircraft the Naxos Z (FuG 350) homer, designed to pick up transmissions from the H2S radar in British bombers, was installed in the Bf 109G-6/N. As this equipment required an antenna in a clear plastic bubble aft of the cockpit, the D/F loop

A Bf 109G prepares to take off with a pair of launchers for Wgr 21 rockets slung under the wing. These were variants of an artillery rocket, unguided and not particularly accurate, and the drag they caused degraded the 109's performance. However, they carried a much larger warhead than any cannon round, and they could cripple an American heavy bomber with a single hit. *(BA)*

was relocated below the fuselage. Although several units operated the Bf 109 as a nocturnal interceptor, NJG 11 apparently received all the Bf 109G-6/Ns that were converted. Other Bf 109s operated in the freelance *Wilde Sau* role under which fighters patrolled over the target areas, attacking bombers silhouetted against the glow of the fires their bombs had caused.

In the East the *Luftwaffe* fighter units led a nomadic existence, gradually being driven back towards the Reich. They could do little to counter the awesome Soviet summer offensive, which saw the destruction of Army Group Centre. The Red Air Force had improved greatly, with excellent Russian fighters such as the Yak 9 and La 5 being more than capable of destroying a 109. But the best of the German *Experten* still had the edge. Dieter Hrabak, who finished the war with a score of 125 in more than 1,000 missions, remembers:

"When I joined JG 52 in November 1942 the unit had scored 4,000 victories. Two years later,

in October 1944, it had 10,000. Men such as Barkhorn, Bartz, Rall, Hartmann and others all had 150 victories. Many other excellent pilots who flew with the *Geschwader* had 100 kills."

And in the East the *Jagdflieger* were far from alone. More Axis units flew in support of the Germans on that front than any other. Spaniards, Rumanians, Italians, Slovakians and Hungarians manned Bf 109s, usually as extra *Staffeln* attached to regular *Luftwaffe* units. Rumanian pilots acquitted themselves particularly well before changing sides as the Red Army threatened to engulf their country in mid-1944. Likewise Hungary and Slovakia changed sides as German fortunes waned, air combat occasionally leading to Bf 109 units skirmishing with their former allies. Finland was also persuaded to become an ally of Russia following the armistice of September 1944, by which time the Allied pincers were closing on Germany from both East and West.

Having been shot to pieces attempting to

A night scene, probably posed for propaganda purposes, nevertheless shows Bf 109Fs at cockpit readiness for a typical *Wilde Sau* take off. More Bf 109s flew night interceptions than is perhaps generally realised, and with some success against the RAF heavy bombers silhouetted against the burning German cities below.

shield the Seventh Army in its retreat from France, the *Jagdwaffe's* casualties reached crippling proportions. Italy had finally proved indefensible from the air, and by the autumn the last German units had departed, leaving air defence in the hands of the Aeronautica Nationale Repubblicana (ANR) which had received its first Bf 109s in May that year.

But by December the Allied advance in the West had slowed, hampered by bad weather. Hitler seized his chance and counterattacked in the Ardennes. The Battle of the Bulge saw the *Jagdwaffe* deployed in a strength not seen on the Western Front for months. Bf 109 and Fw 190 *Gruppen* briefly tasted a few moments of victory, but their success was too localised, too limited and far too reliant on bad weather. Once the conditions improved on 23 December the Allied air forces were back over the contested front line area in force and numerous German fighter units, some equipped with the final Bf 109K-4 variant, again experienced the familiar catalogue of dead, wounded and missing pilots, losses which continued to eat into remaining strength.

Operation *Bodenplatte*, the New Year's Day 1945 attack on Allied airfields in Belgium and Holland, was ostensibly to support operations in the Ardennes. It made little tactical sense unless it could wipe out hundreds of Allied pilots, something the Germans could hardly guarantee. The results were the destruction of aircraft that the Allies could easily replace – and the loss of many of the *Jagdwaffe's* best pilots, who could not be replaced.

By February 1945 the *Luftwaffe* fighter force had been hunted to virtual extinction. Outnumbered, outmanoeuvred and out-gunned, it was crippled by lack of fuel.

Suicide attacks

Even so, fighters could still be marshalled for special operations. On 7 April Goering endorsed a measure that seemed to have been inspired by Japanese kamikazes. At Stendal, the fanatical young pilots of *Sonderkommando Elbe* received rudimentary tuition on the Bf 109. Each individual was simply to take off, climb to altitude – and deliberately ram his fighter into an American bomber.

A Mustang gun-camera view of a Messerschmitt Bf 109 being destroyed. The *Luftwaffe* started the war with better aircraft and better-trained pilots than its adversaries. By 1944, the advent of the P-51 Mustang and other Allied fighters meant that the German fighter force could not control the skies over its own air bases. *(USAF)*

On 7 April, 184 Bf 109s took off and duly climbed to intercept a combined B-17 and B-24 formation. Harried into their targets by P-51s, many of the would-be heroes perished before they came within range. The operation was a disaster for the Germans, who lost as many as forty fighters. The 8th Air Force estimated that only eight out of eighteen bombers lost that day were downed by ramming.

More conventional sorties were carried out by pilots of units such as JG 53, still flying the Bf 109 in the West as it had all through the war. Even to take off could be virtual suicide for the pilots, but most continued to do so, despite there being little in the way of ground control left by that time. A 'fighting retreat' into Czech territory took place under *Luflottenkommando* 6. By 3 May 1945, Bf 109 units had joined bomber, transport and liaison units on bases in that country, where some of the final fighter combats of the war took place as the former Eastern and Western fronts came together.

The German protectorate had avoided much in the way of aerial action during the war, the occupying power establishing flying schools and pressing Czech industry into service. Bf 109s were built at a branch of WNF at Tisnov as early as August 1944, eight aircraft per day being produced in bomb-proof railway tunnels. Avia also tooled up to build Bf 109G-14s although this facility had hardly had time to get into its stride before the Germans were forced to evacuate Prague.

Tightening noose

German fighters were far from safe even in Czechoslovakia, as USAAF fighters flying bomber escort missions were quite capable of combat that far from their bases in England, France and Italy. With their own airfields becoming increasingly untenable and those in Eastern Europe systematically falling to the Red Army, the Germans began basing aircraft across the border in the puppet state of Slovakia where airfield facilities were generally intact. That changed somewhat as Allied intelligence became aware of these relocations and the facilities were bombed by American heavies.

The continual reorganisation of the *Luftwaffe* fighter force as a result of attrition saw the

A late-war picture of a Bf 109G-10, which has been fitted with a clear-view *Erla Haube* canopy. In capable hands, the 109 was still able to hold its own against any foe, but by the start of 1945 attrition and the pressures of years of non-stop combat had whittled down the numbers of *Experten*, and most pilots were novices. *(BA)*

Bf 109 being operated in an expanded short range reconnaissance role in support of the army. Usually consisting of one or more *Staffeln* rather than full *Gruppen*, these NAGr units were among the last to fly German-manned Bf 109 sorties in both Italy and central Europe.

Final air battles

A week before the cessation of hostilities, on 3 May 1945, *Luftkdo* 6 encompassed six NAGr formations as well as the *Stab.* and II./JG 77 and the *Stab.* and I./JG 52, which was complete apart from 1./*Staffel*. In addition *Luftwaffen Gefechtsverband Weiss* had 2./NAGr 2 as its sole subordinate unit and *Gefechtsverband Rudel's* sizeable command consisted of the *Stab* and 1. and 2./ NAGr 15 as well as 7.(Erg) JG 1, all of which operated versions of the Bf 109G.

Some of the long established fighter *Geschwadern* that had been expanded and added a fourth *Gruppe* in the mid-war years now found such a lack of pilots that they lost component *Gruppen* or were merged with others. JG 54, for example, largely combined with JG 26 for the last few months of hostilities.

Some of the disbanded units had literally been wiped out.

In the West, pilots of the remaining Bf 109 *Geschwadern* still encountered fighters of the RAF, their antagonist for close on six years of warfare. April 1945 saw the last combats between these 'traditional' enemies, III./JG 26 coming into contact on several occasions, mainly with Typhoons and Tempests. The differences between the two Hawker fighters was academic to the Germans, and on 4 April the *Geschwader* filed claims for two Tempests when its victims were actually Typhoons of No 438 Sqn RCAF. On the 20th a Bf 109 destroyed a Spitfire IX of No 401 Sqn RCAF, the report of this combat being the last to specifically mention the Messerschmitt fighter.

With few resources left, surviving German fighter units which still had some structure were ordered to destroy their aircraft to prevent them falling intact into the hands of Allied ground forces. In numerous cases personnel simply abandoned their aircraft before melting away. By 8 May the majority of the fighter *Geschwader* had formally surrendered.

3. Engineers and *Experten*: 109 People

In designing the Bf 109, Willy Messerschmitt incorporated much of his considerable experience with lightweight, unpowered airframes. The BFW company had little experience in designing military aircraft and the Bf 108 was the closest it came – a modern liaison aircraft with a stressed skin monocoque structure. While fully aware of the stresses that military flying imposed, Messerschmitt tended to underestimate the advances in aircraft weaponry and opted for high performance to the detriment of heavy firepower. More guns would have severely compromised his fighter and perhaps led to the need for a more powerful – and perhaps heavier – engine. The weight-performance conundrum that every aircraft designer has to confront sooner or later leads inevitably to compromises.

The decade of the 1930s was extremely stimulating for the industry but at the halfway point much of the promise inherent in new powerplants, systems and armament was tinged with uncertainties. Only time would tell if engines were as reliable as early bench runs and prototype tests appeared to indicate – Messerschmitt was not alone in having his prototype fighter ready to fly before there was an engine to power it. But by saving weight in fixed armament the Bf 109 was somewhat compromised from the outset and in the opinion of some commentators this was never satisfactorily addressed.

The wing firepower problem had been overcome by the time the Bf 109E-3 appeared and for a brief period the ' Emil' model's twin 20-mm wing cannon and two fuselage-mounted 7.9-mm machine guns made it one of the world's most heavily armed fighters.

But this extra lethality was not bought without cost; saddling the Emil with a heavier engine, armour protection and additional ammunition stowage inevitably resulted in a higher wing-loading. The landing speed consequently went up and brought about a worrying increase in Bf 109E crashes and ground loops. But with major air operations in Western Europe looming it was expedient to retain the cannon in the wing of the E series.

Sleeker but weaker

In the general airframe 'clean up' he performed on the Bf 109 to create the F, Messerschmitt was perhaps a shade too radical or preoccupied to give the new model the close scrutiny it required. It soon became clear that the stresses imposed on the cantilever tailplane, which had been borne by strut supports on the Bf 109E, had not been thoroughly evaluated.

When the Bf 109F was delivered to front line units the tailplane weakness resulted in a number of aircraft being lost under certain flight conditions. Messerschmitt had to contend with a telegram sent by *Feldmarschall* Albert Kesselring, C-in-C of *Luftflotte* 2, to the effect that he had refused to permit any further use of the Bf 109F until the tailplane weakness had been cured.

A temporary remedy was to weld strengthening plates across the fuselage-tail junction prior to further internal strengthening,

Professor Willy Messerschmitt congratulates company test pilot Fritz Wendel, seated in the cockpit of the Me 209 V1 after achieving a new world speed record on 26 April 1939. The German propaganda machine attributed the feat to a version of the Bf 109, which successfully enhanced the fighter's reputation. *(IWM)*

but Kesselring's criticism of the F series did not end with one telegram. On 4 April he complained to Udet of several more deficiencies in the aircraft, including the positioning of the pilot's seat which was too far forward so that an occupant wearing full flying kit could not move the stick back far enough to carry out a three-point landing. Further cited were deformation of the wings in high-G manoeuvres, excessive tyre wear, wide variations in fuel consumption and, as before, the generally weak aft fuselage junction.

Messerschmitt addressed these problems and the Bf 109F was improved, although that did not silence its critics. A number of pilots, citing its weak armament, put off flying it for as long as was possible. Factory modifications inevitably caused some late deliveries of the improved F series, which did not of course sit well with the high command.

Training

Training hundreds of fighter pilots to fly the Bf 109 was a challenge which the *Luftwaffe* handled well enough in the last years of peace. The Condor Legion's operations in the Spanish Civil War were practical demonstrations of a tactical doctrine based around fast reaction to a crisis and concentrated use of overwhelming force to secure an objective. Under the energetic command of Wolfram von Richthofen, cousin of the famous WWI ace, the Legion flourished and became a formidable fighting force that nurtured a generation of German fighter pilots.

Werner Mölders returned from Spain with a respectable sixteen victories, a score that made

Ehrhard Milch, one of the creators of the *Luftwaffe*, speaks to two of its outstanding personalities. The flamboyant, mustachioed Adolf Galland flew with a Mickey Mouse emblem on his Bf 109 and had an ash tray in the cockpit for his ever-present cigars. The clean-cut Werner Mölders was a complete contrast – a quiet, serious Catholic who was nevertheless an outstanding tactician and leader of men. *(US National Archives)*

him the Legion's most successful fighter pilot. Next came Wolfgang Schellmann with twelve and Harro Harder with eleven. Such combat experience immeasurably helped the training process, and the knowledge the 'Spaniards' had gained was put to good use.

It was after World War II began and combat casualties gradually rose that intensified training created difficulties. Cadets converting onto the Bf 109 at the *Jagdfliegerschulen* (Fighter Pilots' Training Schools) found that no trainer could quite duplicate the power to weight ratio of the Bf 109, or its tricky, narrow track landing gear and steep ground angle which provided only a limited forward view when taxying.

The *Luftwaffe* made no provision for its fighter pilots to fly operational tours with a set number of sorties or a given period of time. Instead the approach was that under the original 'short war' policy, an individual flew for as long as he might be needed for the duration of a campaign. Everthing was geared

Adolf Galland pictured in the captured RAF Irvin flying suit trousers which helped keep the cold out on winter sorties across the Channel. Midway through the war Galland was called on to fight the *Jagdwaffe's* battles from behind a desk when he became Inspector and then General of *Jagdflieger*.

to the front line and offensive operations, with a large scale training programme that could supply pilots for a prolonged conflict being virtually ignored.

Short, victorious wars

Fortunately for Germany, the early campaigns of World War II in Poland, Norway and Western Europe were of surprisingly short duration, after which fighter pilots could be rested for brief periods. Many veterans recall that the winter of 1940/41 was the only time that they enjoyed a leave period of any length during the war years. Thereafter leave was counted in single days rather than weeks.

Several Replacement Fighter Groups or *Ergänzungsjagdgruppen* were established, usually attached to the front line fighter *Jagdgeschwadern* to make good operational losses. The role of these units took on an increasing importance when the conflict widened to encompass the Soviet Union.

Experienced pilots were required as instructors, as the demand for fighter pilots rose steadily. This duty was looked upon as rest of a kind. Before the war the *Luftwaffe* had established a well trained cadre of officers, many gaining a vast amount of operational experience. However, combat attrition meant that there was a high risk of these pilots being killed or badly wounded the longer they remained in the front line. The cracks in the system were beginning to show even after the *Kanalkampf*; exhausted by the daily sorties, the *Jagdflieger* carried out their task well but not without the loss of many experienced men.

By late 1940, the number of replacement pilots required by the operational *Gruppen* began eating into what reserve there was, with the result that entry standards for new cadets were gradually lowered.

Irrespective of the outcome, the battles over Britain elevated such individuals as Adolf Galland, Helmut Wick and Walter Oesau to widespread fame throughout the fighter arm and to public acclaim in the Reich itself.

The *Kanalkampf* ended on a very sour note for the *Jagdwaffe* on 28 November 1940 when Wick, then the force's leading *Experte*, was shot down in combat with Spitfires. Having scored 56 victories, Wick should have been rested by that

Leading Fortress killer Egon Mayer of JG 2. He commanded III *Gruppe* from November 1942 until 30 June 1943. Proficient on both the Bf 109 and the Fw 190, Meyer's knack of getting in close enough to destroy the American heavies was ably demonstrated on 6 September 1943 when he shot down three B-17s in the space of 19 minutes. Meyer was killed on 2 March 1944 after being bounced by P-47s. *(BA)*

time. However, the somewhat restrictive German system was not entirely to blame for fatigued pilots – in common with many of his fellows, being taken off operations would probably have been anathema to Wick. But it did place enormous responsibility in the hands of the high scoring *Experten* who became the cement that held the entire *Jagdwaffe* together.

As German fortunes waned, the degree of combat the fighter units faced and the quality of their adversaries varied. Even so, pilots faced a gruelling regime of continuous service, often lasting for years. This situation could bring an individual a steadily increasing log of combat successes, so much so that the records of opposing Allied pilots looked very meagre by comparison. Under their high risk system, several individual German pilots accumulated scores superior to those achieved by entire squadrons of Allied fighters.

More flights, more kills

If these aerial victory scores were examined on any basis other than purely numerical, the comparisons with their Allied counterparts were hardly valid. German pilots simply flew more combat missions – up to 2,000 in some cases, compared with the 30 or 40 flown by Americans on a combat tour. These drawbacks did not seem to have much adverse effect on the German pilots themselves, the *Jagdflieger* maintaining a remarkable *esprit de corps*. War flying brought its own momentum, which endured even after Hitler's death.

In six years of combat Bf 109 pilots claimed more enemy aircraft in aerial combat than any

Werner Mölders emerged as one of the most consistently successful Bf 109 fighter pilots, having scored the highest number of kills in Spain and raising his total to 65 by the end of 1940. This is his personal Bf 109F-2 probably seen at Wiesbaden, early in 1941. *(IWM)*

other comparable force. Heading the long list was Erich Hartmann with 352 victories, followed by Gerhard Barkhorn with 301. Next came the thirteen members of the '200 club' the leader of which was Gunther Rall with 275, followed by twenty who were credited with 150 or more. Pilots who claimed victories in double figures ran into multiple hundreds.

Awards

Germany had a fairly loose system of awarding medals for aerial victories. In 1940, a pilot could be considered an *Experte* with a baseline score of ten. In those early days, the highly-coveted *Ritterkreuz* (Knight's Cross or RK) was awarded for much lower scores than were to be common later – Werner Mölders was awarded the first *Luftwaffe* RK of the war on 27 May 1940 when his personal victory tally stood at 20. Later, the threshold rose to 50 and then 100 kills, though some were awarded to pilots for multiple scores of substantially less than 100 but who had perhaps performed outstanding acts of

bravery and demonstrated exemplary leadership. It was widely known that the *Experten* inspired the rank and file – and that most of a unit's victories tended to accrue to a few outstanding pilots.

After the *Ritterkreuz*, successively higher awards were the Oak Leaves, the Swords and the Diamonds. A fairly typical high scoring recipient was *Oberst* Wolf-Dietrich Wilke, who was awarded the RK for 25 kills, the Oak Leaves for 100 and the Swords when his score reached 155. Wilke's awards were in contrast to those of *Oberleutnant* Otto Kittel, the top-scoring Fw 190 ace, who had shot down 123 enemy aircraft before becoming a *Ritterkreuz-trager* (literally 'Knight's Cross bearer', or holder of the RK). He did not receive the Oak Leaves until his score had risen to 152, and the Swords did not come until he reached 230.

With typical irreverence, the *Jagdflieger* nicknamed their medals, and when a recipient of the RK would go on to be awarded the Oak Leaves, it was dubbed the 'cauliflower'. Pilots

The rudder of Heinz Bar's Bf 109F at Kertsch in Russia on 27 June 1942. Bar then flew as part of the *Stab* of IV./JG 51. Reaching the rank of Major, Bar gained 221 victories over enemy aircraft in more than 1,000 combat missions, and he survived 18 crashes. He ended the war with the *Ritterkreuz des Eisernes Kreuzes mit Eichenlaub und Schwertern* (Knight's Cross of the Iron Cross with Oak Leaves and Swords). *(Crow)*

Unrivalled in his ability to destroy enemy aircraft, in spite of regularly fighting against heavy odds, Hans-Joachim Marseille of JG 27 was dubbed the 'Star of Africa' by the German propaganda machine. He is seen here in one of several Bf 109s marked as 'Yellow 14' flown by him in North Africa. *(BA)*

who appeared eager to claim kills were said to suffer from a 'sore throat' which would only be cured when the ribbon of the distinctive black and silver cross was hung around his neck.

Meeting the Führer

There was an additional bonus in being an award recipient, as the individual usually travelled to Berlin to receive the medal from the Fuhrer's own hands – and a few days' leave, a break from the rigours of front line combat was invariably allowed at the same time.

Before Operation *Barbarossa*, the number of *Ritterkreuztrager* in all branches of the German armed forces had increased steadily, but at a pace that was normal considering the level of wartime operations, the scale of forces under arms and the early German successes in combat. But with the Russian campaign the phenomenal scoring rate by the fighter pilots saw an enormous increase in eligible recipients of the highest award for gallantry.

This proliferation threatened to devalue the Knight's Cross and a system of 'victory points' was introduced. Each different front generated a contrasting number of points for an aerial victory – ground kills were not counted in the *Luftwaffe*. For example, a USAAF heavy bomber garnered four points for the pilot who destroyed it, while a Pe-2 claimed in Russia was deemed to be worth only two.

The Germans did not award 'half', 'quarter' or other percentage shares in a kill to several pilots who may have opened fire on the same enemy aircraft, but credited the victory to the unit. This was probably a fair solution to the multiple claims that could arise in the frequent confusion of air combat. Not that an element of luck, being in the right place at the right time, did not play its part. Numerous good pilots had to wait months, if not years for success in air combat to come their way.

Scores continued to accrue to a select band of *Experten* but combat inevitably took its toll even of the best pilots, and as the experienced pre-war trained flyers began to disappear, the quality of the rank and file *Luftwaffe* pilots steadily dropped. After the heady victories of 1940-41 the *Jagdwaffe* never fully recovered from the effects of continual attrition and by 1944 pilot quality was inevitably suffering from reduced training times.

Still, the leading Bf 109 *Experten* such as Walter Shuck, Eric Hartmann, Gunther Rall and Dieter Hrabak soldiered on, leading a flock that was ever changing as inexperienced pilots were quickly lost and replaced. Inexorably, cadet training time had to be curtailed further when fuel shortages began to take effect. Survival for some of the top *Experten* sometimes seemed to hinge on the length of time spent away from the front line. Hermann Graf, who served with *Jagdgruppe* 50 for some years before joining JG 52 to eventually accumulate 202 victories, was used on home-front propaganda tours, and spent some time in hospital before returning to command JG 52 at the end of 1944.

Gunther Rall was among the men who were obliged to convalesce after being wounded in action; downed in November 1941 he did not return to JG 52 until August the following year but soon showed that the enforced rest had not blunted his skills. Rall was quickly back on the road that would culminate in his place as Germany's third highest scoring fighter pilot with 275 kills.

Disaster front

That the *Jagdflieger* operating in Russia were fighting an entirely different kind of war to their colleagues in the West was starkly brought home to units when they were transferred, whereupon their losses tended to spiral. The Eastern Front may have been a dread posting to German ground troops but to the airmen it was, despite its deprivations, nothing compared to the bloody slugging match with the American escorts over the country's shattered cities. The Red Air Force had virtually no strategic bomber force and the generally shorter ranges over which combat took place suited the German fighter pilots, especially those flying the Bf 109 with its limited endurance.

In the West everything became geared to bolstering the front line fighter units but the

One of the *Luftwaffe's* most famous *Experten* was Johannes Trautloft of JG 54 *Grunhertz*. He chose the unit's 'Green Heart' insignia to recall his home in Thuringia, first applying the device to one of the Bf 109 *Versuchs* machines he flew in Spain.

Hans-Joachim Marseille watches the *Staffel* painter apply the finishing touches to the fiftieth kill marker on the rudder of his Bf 109F. Note the ten-kill stencil by the latter's knee. Following this victory, Marseille was awarded the *Ritterkreuz* on 24 February 1942.

number of experienced pilots gradually dwindled to the point that resistance to the mighty Allied air fleets was a mere gesture of defiance. Sending barely-trained boys against an enemy who was stronger in terms of striking power in 1944-45 than the entire *Luftwaffe* had ever been in its heyday, was bound to be little short of catastrophic.

Outclassed by the Allies

That the Bf 109 was almost totally eclipsed by Allied fighters in the West was demonstrated on numerous occasions; published comparison figures clearly indicated that the German fighter, compared to the later Spitfires and Tempest V, the P-51D and P-47M, was inferior on most counts. Events occasionally proved this to be a dangerous assumption, as any aircraft is only as good as the man at the controls. Allied pilots on bomber escort duty could still report a hard fight with an obviously well seasoned

opponent - but from their point of view the *Jagdflieger* often found themselves facing not a section of four enemy aircraft but whole squadrons of fresh, well-trained pilots.

On the defensive

Aerial engagements could be remarkably one-sided in 1944-45, and the reason the *Luftwaffe* lost so heavily must surely lie in the vulnerability of German fighters to Allied aerial guns. Although the Bf 109G had head and back armour protection for the pilot, a 'broadside' from the 0.50-in machine guns (six or eight for the Mustang and Thunderbolt respectively), or the cannon armament of the Spitfire and Tempest, was often more than enough to fatally weaken the lightweight structure or blow the Messerschmitt apart. Even if he was not wounded, a pilot could hardly take evasive action if his aircraft had taken terminal airframe damage, and recovery was next to impossible. Fire, that most deadly of air combat occurrences, also overtook the Bf 109 on frequent occasions although the aircraft had no greater propensity to burn than its contemporaries. In a crash landing the lightweight frame of the Bf 109 tended to break up, with the fuselage often splitting just aft of the cockpit leaving the pilot's position intact.

The deceptively simple matter of relative skill was overshadowed by the kind of war the *Jagdwaffe* was fighting. Being totally outnumbered was daunting in the extreme, and the knowledge that a whole flight of Bf 109s could be shot down in seconds when bounced by enemy fighters became a daily burden. In such circumstances, a number of German pilots exercised the 'live to fight another day' option and simply bailed out when attacked.

The *Jagdflieger*'s options were few in a fighter versus bomber engagement. The Bf 109G had to get through the escort fighter cordon and be skilfully manoeuvred and positioned to make maximum use of its cannon and machine guns. The pilot had to remember to charge the guns and keep a close check on the cockpit round counters to ensure that sufficient ammunition was available and not expend it before the target was in range. This happened on frequent occasions, as there was a basic self-preservation instinct to open fire just slightly beyond the

Walter Dahl's record in the *Luftwaffe* included 128 victories, 77 of them in the East. Originally an instructor pilot, he did not see combat until 1941, and ended the war flying Me 262 jets. His career was notable for Hermann Goering's threat to have him shot for 'insubordination'– which probably meant that the outspoken Dahl talked the kind of plain common sense that the *Reichsmarschall* did not want to hear. (BA)

range of the bombers' defensive fire. This phenomenon, widely known as *Jagerschreck*, was hard for some individuals to overcome.

A pilot approaching an American bomber formation would usually select a combat box of say, ten B-17s. The bombers would be defended by at least 100 fifty-calibre machine guns, over half of them in powered positions. The Browning had a stopping power midway between a rifle-calibre machine gun bullet and a cannon round, and was a very capable weapon. From his point of view the *Jagdflieger*

needed to close right in to use his cannon effectively. Although a wingman was *de rigueur* in combat, aircraft often got separated and individual attacks were by no means uncommon – but the disadvantage the German pilot operated under can be fully appreciated. Widely circulated official *Luftwaffe* bulletins extolled pilots to stringently follow the cardinal rule and always get in close. It was much easier said than done.

If the air war demanded a new generation of pilots of the quality that the *Luftwaffe* could no

Hauptmann Ernst Düllberg poses by his Bf 109 after being made *Gruppenkommodore* of III JG.27 in North Africa. Düllberg scored 45 kills, including ten *Viermots* or four-engined heavies. He scored JG 27's 2,000th kill of the war, a Spitfire shot down over the Greek Islands in September 1943. *(BA)*

longer find, numerous fighter pilots lived long enough to become highly decorated national heroes. In the West, it was the *Viermot Experten*, those men able to shoot down multiple American heavy bombers, who received the accolades. This was totally justified as the B-17 was particularly robust and capable of absorbing a degree of battle damage that was a surprise to friend and foe alike. Egon Mayer of JG 2 was one pilot who made a habit of downing B-17s. Renowned as the 'Fortress Specialist' Mayer accounted for 25 of the big Boeings (as the Germans often called them) before losing his life on 2 March 1944. Only three other pilots (Werner Schroer, Hermann Staiger and Hugo Frey) beat Mayer in this respect and then only by one bomber apiece. Several other pilots ran their Fortress scores into double figures, while others shot down B-24 Liberators. However, the Consolidated bomber was less frequently encountered before the advent of US long-range fighter escorts.

Combat in Russia demanded a different discipline. Although things were relatively easy for the *Jagdflieger,* he was occasionally exposed to the desperate threat of *tarom,* or ramming. Opposition was provided by such capable types as the diminutive I-16 and the Yakovlev, MiG and Lavochkin single-seaters, which were highly manoeuvrable and armed similarly to the Bf 109. Destroying the incredibly tough Il-2, the *Shturmovik,* was a serious challenge. Very well armoured, the Il-2 could absorb a remarkable degree of battle damage. It took a dedicated German fighter pilot to seek out the Russian aircraft's weak underside areas if he was to score a certain victory.

Mediterranean opposition

On the southern front, the *Jagdflieger* was liable to come up against numerous RAF aircraft, including the first American Lend-Lease types encountered in force. While the British fighters were familiar foes, the combat capability of the

P-40 Warhawk/Kittyhawk and P-38 Lightning was relatively unknown. Occasionally they proved to be relatively easy meat for a well handled Bf 109, and the big twin-engined P-38 with its distinctive twin-boom configuration could be recognised at some distance.

JG 27's *Hauptmann* Hans-Joachim Marseille will always be associated with the early days of the desert war, and his remarkable scoring rate against western opposition, including the feat of 17 destroyed in a single day's combat, was unequalled. Excellent tactics pressed home aggressively saw Marseille and other Bf 109 pilots run up impressive personal scores in North Africa and over Malta before Allied numbers inevitably began to tell and the demands of other theatres of war drew German fighters away from the area. By mid-1943 Italian ambitions in the Mediterranean were in ruins and the *Jagdwaffe* was forced to all but abandon the area as the defence of the homeland demanded ever more resources.

On all fronts

The progress of the war would result in some Bf 109 units fighting on all fronts at different times. The policy of detaching one or more constituent units to deal with a localised threat often resulted in the three or four *Gruppen* in any *Geschwader* operating apart for many months, if not years. Adolf Galland, the hard-working *General der Jagdflieger*, tried to rectify this anomaly and to keep units together.

The sheer scale of the air fighting on every front during 1944 totally disrupted the German fighter arm – as the USAAF Pointblank plan had intended. Hunted from production line to front line airfield, in aerial combat and on the ground, German fighters were lost in their hundreds in the months leading up to D-Day. Through their enormous tactical offensive in North West Europe the Allies succeeded in forcing the *Jagdwaffe* so completely onto the defensive that Operation *Overlord* was unlikely to be seriously contested.

For their part the Germans pulled most of their fighters out of France to prevent their utter destruction. The *Luftwaffe* high command gambled everything on the fighter and flak defences of the homeland being strong enough to eventually deter the Allies from continuing

Unlike Allied pilots, who kept score on the fuselage beneath the cockpit, *Luftwaffe* aces invariably recorded their triumphs on the rudder. This Bf 109F was flown by Sigfried Schnell when he was *Staffelkapitan* of 9./JG 2, based at Theville, France at the end of May 1942. (BA)

their bomber offensive. Given the heavy fighter losses in the previous two years, that hope seemed very remote indeed, but many were buoyed up by the continuous production miracles wrought by the aircraft industry which maintained the supply, particularly of Bf 109s, to the fighting units.

Attrition bites hard

The effects of combat attrition removing some of the leading *Experten* spread through the fighter force; such men were renowned and well known, with their exploits widely recorded in publications such as the German

One of the many bright stars of JG 52 was Johannes Steinhoff, pictured here in his Messerschmitt 'office' when he was *Gruppenkommandeur* of II./JG 52 in the Crimea in 1942. Dreadfully burned in an accident with an Me 262 at the end of the war, Steinhoff survived to become a general in the post war *Bundesluftwaffe*. *(Crow)*

propaganda journal *Signal* and in radio broadcasts. But those who followed found circumstances vastly changed, an atmosphere where dogged determination was no substitute for experience. It was increasingly difficult for them to emulate the pilots who had made the *Luftwaffe* the successful force it had been in the early war years.

Against the odds

The period after D-Day became a terrible time of martyrdom for the *Jagdflieger*. At first, the rapid response to Operation *Overlord* appeared sound, with the High Command despatching fifteen *Jagdgruppen*, eleven of them flying Bf 109s, to northwestern France as a counter invasion force . It was not. Faced with an Allied fighter superiority of as much as 20 to 1, the *Jagdwaffe* could achieve next to nothing. One of the problems was that the Germans sent their aircraft on fighter-bomber missions against troops, vehicles and shipping. Faced with hazardous low flying, the Bf 109 pilots, who had been trained in bomber interception, were at a disadvantage. One hundred and seventy were lost in the last three weeks of June 1944 alone. Qualified individuals were continually recalled from staff desks or instructor posts to help shore up the sagging fronts until, in many cases, they too fell in action.

Powerless to hamper the Allies driving the German Army out of France, the *Luftwaffe* fighter force had all but disappeared from those skies by the autumn of 1944. Unsuited to a ground attack role even if they could penetrate the Allied tactical fighter shield, the Bf 109

Overall third ranking German fighter ace Gunther Rall poses with his Bf 109E 'White 10' when he was serving with 8./JG 52 on the Channel coast. Along with Hartmann and Barkhorn, the top two aces, Rall went on to become a jet commander when the *Luftwaffe* was reborn in the 1950s. *(Crow)*

Gruppen in the West soon returned to Germany to concentrate their efforts on bomber interception – until they were given a new, desperate mission. A winter lull broken by the Ardennes offensive saw an increase in *Jagdwaffe* sorties by a carefully marshalled force of Bf 109s and Fw 190s – but fighter casualties rose once the weather cleared in late December.

Operation *Bodenplatte*

Units were alerted for a special ground attack operation on the morning of 1 January 1945. Hundreds of Bf 109s and Fw 190s took off to raid Allied fighter bases in Holland and Belgium, and those pilots who found their targets pressed home their attacks. The resulting smoke columns attested to what looked like a successful operation, but when

heads were counted back at the bases there were far too many empty chairs. Operation *Bodenplatte*, the *Jagdwaffe's* last desperate gamble, had failed.

And yet, as the *Luftwaffe* resigned itself to the inevitable, the air war went on. Eric Hartmann scored his 352nd kill on 8 May when he destroyed a Yak 7 over Brunn. Almost as impressive as his kill record was the fact that Hartmann had completed 1,405 combat operations and been involved in 825 aerial engagements since he was posted to III./JG 52 on the Eastern Front on 10 October 1942.

One might argue that Hartmann was an exceptionally skilled pilot – but in the *Jagdwaffe* he was far from alone. Even if 'Bubi's' colleagues did not quite reach his unmatchable position as the most successful fighter pilot in

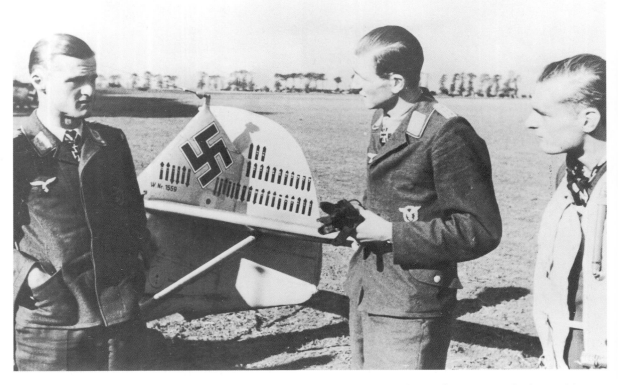

This trio of *Experten* includes (l to r) Gunther Lutzow (*Kommodore* of JG 3) Wilhelm Balthasar (*Gruppenkommandeur*) and Egon Troha (*Staffelkapitan* of 9./JG 3). The tail of the Bf 109E (WNr 1559) is that of Balthasar's personal aircraft which he brought with him on transferring from JG 1. (IWM)

history, there were those whose scores were almost as impressive. Such a record as Hartmann's is proof that a Bf 109 in skilled hands remained a deadly weapon from the first missions on 1 September 1939 right up until the last day of the war.

End of a long war

In the end, a combination of factors led to the defeat of the *Luftwaffe*. Added together, these proved more than enough to neutralise a force that simply had not been sufficiently modernised in terms of aircraft, had not built up a strong reserve in the event of a protracted war and had failed to establish an effective pilot training programme to meet long term requirements. The *Luftwaffe* had been created to fight short *Blitzkrieg* campaigns in support of the *Wehrmacht*, and it found itself in a war of attrition with three of the world's great powers.

While the Germans fielded weapons of outstanding quality, and in the case of the Bf 109 maintained deliveries in vast quantities under the most difficult of circumstances, the human element was fatally neglected. The failure of the *Luftwaffe* leadership to make that allowance resulted in its dedicated and highly skilled pilots paying the penalty, hundreds of times over. In the final analysis all the Bf 109 *Jagdgeschwader* had aquitted themselves well in combat despite overwhelming odds that had claimed the lives of so many.

Those fighter pilots who survived the war were justifiably relieved. They had flown hundreds, even thousands of missions, and most had been shot down several times and few had escaped wounds. But for many who fought in the East, there was the additional burden of being an unwilling guest of the Russians for several years.

4. Combat Zone:
The 109's Accomplishments

An elegant, angular monoplane with clean, uncluttered lines, the Bf 109 made a highly favourable impression when it first appeared in 1935. Quite futuristic when compared to the fighter biplanes then in *Luftwaffe* service, Willy Messerschmitt's creation personified high speed and it was this attribute that was exploited during the prestigious Zurich flying meeting at Dubendorf in the summer of 1937.

Germany publicly unveiled several new aircraft at the event, and entered five Bf 109s – four prototypes and a B-1. Prior to the Zurich meeting, BFW fitted a Daimler-Benz DB 601A engine in the Bf 109 V13 (D-IPKY). While this 'racing engine' was intended purely for competition, its performance gave the manufacturer useful pointers to the future. A second Zurich participant, Bf 109 V14 (D-ISLU) also had a DB 601, a Rennmotor II with a maximum output rated at 1,565 hp at 2,620 rpm. It drove a three-bladed VDM airscrew.

During the ten-day meeting the German fighter performed brilliantly. Carl Francke of the *E-Stelle* at Rechlin captured the four-lap 125 mile (202 km) circuit race in the Bf 109 V7, after Ernst Udet in the Bf 109 V14 was forced to withdraw with engine trouble. Francke's average speed was 254.59 mph (409.64 km/h) at an elapsed time of 29 minutes, 35.2 seconds.

Udet's aircraft was ready for the Alpine Circuit on 1 July, this consisting of a 77.68 mile (125 km) course from Dubendorf via Thun and Bellinzona and back to Dubendorf. Germany beat four Czechoslovak and one French aircraft,

but not before Udet had crash-landed and written off the V 14. The event was won by Major Sidemann flying the Bf 109 V9, in 56 minutes, 47.1 seconds. In the Alpine Circuit event for three aircraft flying the course in formation, the Bf 109s were again successful with a time of 58 minutes, 52.9 seconds. Finally, Francke flew the Bf 109 V13 for the international climb and dive competition. Competitors were required to climb to 13,124 ft (4 000 m) over Dubendorf and then dive, aiming at a target stripe and pulling out at 3,280 ft (1 000 m). Francke won, adopting steep dive angles of 70-75 degrees during his 2 minutes, 5.7 second attempt.

Record breaking Bf 109

In capturing several pre-war speed records, the Bf 109 indelibly stamped itself on the pages of aviation history. Even if the aircraft had then faded from the scene, such records stand in perpetuity. Inspired by the success at Zurich, BFW decided to make an attempt on the world speed record as classified by the FAI as Category C, landplanes.

After Zurich the Bf 109 V13 was readied for the record. A Rennmotor III engine was installed, a modified DB 601A rated at 1,660 hp. Setting a new record with a speed of 379.38 mph (610.950 km/h) the Bf 109 was officially certificated to that effect as the 'Bf 113R'.

Although this record decisively beat that set previously by the USA with 352.39 mph (567.115 km/h), Germany wanted to widen the gap even further. This was not achieved with

On 4 December 1937, one of the first production Bf 109Bs was forced down behind Republican lines in Spain. Evaluated by a French mission, the test pilot's report was suppressed for diplomatic reasons, and information which could have been valuable in 1940 never reached the French air force.

the Bf 109, however, despite several attempts. By modifying the prototype Me 209 Germany later raised the absolute record to 469.22 mph (755.138 km/h) but the fact that the aircraft was not a variant of the Bf 109 was not widely appreciated at the time. As a result, the achievement appeared to enhance still further the reputation of Germany's much vaunted single-seater. Thanks to a little opportunist subterfuge, Messerschmitt had more than put his fighter on the map.

Forged in Spain

The fine record of the Bf 109 with *Jagdgruppe* 88 in Spain boosted *Luftwaffe* confidence not only in the quality of German arms, but in an entirely new advance in tactical airpower. Utilising the performance of the Bf 109 in intelligent and practical formations paid dividends during the civil war, where the Germans were up against Republican pilots who though skilled, were hampered by a variety of international aircraft types with differing performance. Despite its lightweight gun power the early Bf 109 had little difficulty

in despatching Republican bombers such as the SB 2, although pilots could find themselves in a difficult situation if they met the nimble Russian I-16 with a good pilot at the controls.

With the advent of the Bf 109E, the *Jagdwaffe* received a fighter with an outstanding overall performance, easily the equal of any of the contemporary fighters then in service .

With the almost inevitable outbreak of war on 1 September 1939, the *Luftwaffe* was unleashed on Poland. There, the few *Gruppen* of Bf 109s committed to the battle had little opportunity to indulge in large scale air combat. This situation prevailed for several more months with the transition to the 'Phoney War' in the West. For the attack on Norway only a single *Gruppe* of Bf 109s was deployed, and these continued to take a shared role in *Luftwaffe* operations to secure the country.

However, the Messerschmitt *Jagdflieger* took centre stage on 10 May 1940 when the *Wehrmacht* unleashed its *Blitzkrieg* in the west. Knifing through Belgium, whose first line fighter defence consisted of Hurricanes and 15 Gloster Gladiators, the *Jagdflieger* ensured that

The small size of the Bf 109 meant that routine engine maintenance could be carried out without resort to cumbersome workstands and ladders. Bf 109Es are on the flight line here, the unit probably being LG 2.

very few of these fighters were able to take off. In Holland it was much the same picture. A handful of Fokker D XXIs and G 1s of the Royal Netherlands Air Force were swamped, fighting gallantly but in vain to prevent the Germans over-running the country. Most of the twin-boom Fokkers were destroyed in combat.

Coming up against a miscellany of *Armée de l'Air* fighters, the Bf 109 pilots found the Dewoitine D 520 one of the most worthy adversaries they had yet met in combat. Armed with a centreline cannon and four machine guns, the D 520 saw service with five air force and one naval *Groupe de Chasse* before France capitulated.

British opposition

The Hawker Hurricane Mk Is flown by RAF squadrons in France were as good as the Dewoitines. Although similar to the ill-fated Belgian machines, the British fighters enjoyed much more freedom to fight. But there

The Bf 109 V15, one of the prototypes of the E model, was the third aircraft to be powered by the DB 601. The new powerplant boosted the Bf 109's performance tremendously, and the Emil was to be the backbone of the *Jagdwaffe* through the early, triumphant years of World War Two.

was poor overall military organisation and limited ground control to direct fighters to trouble spots. Having shattered many forward French airfields in the early stages of the fight for North West Europe, the *Luftwaffe* found the French response vested in interception sorties by its most numerous fighter, the MS 406. Having equipped four *Escadres de Chasse*, each of three *Groupes*, by the start of the war, there were enough MS 406s on hand to equip more units before the armistice. It was to little avail.

Dogfighting with elan and skill and indulging in the relatively new form of fighter attack, that of ground strafing, the Bf 109s helped disrupt air support to the French army. Additionally, the enormous psychological advantage that the scent of victory brought the Germans was certainly a factor in their success.

'Free hunting' out across France, the Messerschmitt pilots confirmed that the Hurricane was not without its weak spots – but the outcome of combat invariably depended on the relative positions and size of the opposing forces. The British fighter was heavily armed and its eight MGs provided a good bullet spread, but the Germans could counter that with the greater power of their cannon.

Flushed with the incredible victory over France, the *Luftwaffe*'s young Turks were confident about future combat with the British. Few really appreciated the magnitude of the task they now faced, and a straw poll would have found total belief in another German victory. Failure was not contemplated.

Bf 109 meets its match

Yet failure it was, and in the following months the strongest, most battle-tested air force in the world failed to destroy a smaller number of enemy fighters. The RAF was the first force they had encountered which was fully equipped with aircraft to match the Bf 109 – and the British fighters were backed by a superb early warning system, a carefully planned network of monitoring centres, interlinked airfields and repair centres. Above all, the defending pilots demonstrated a tenacity and determination to win that far outshone anything the *Luftwaffe* had previously encountered. The *Jagdflieger* had to admit that they were often outfought by Hurricanes and Spitfires. More often than not, pride made them claim combat with Spitfires, though the RAF actually flew far more Hurricanes during the Battle of Britain.

In fighter versus fighter dogfights during the

Kanalkampf the Bf 109E's cannon often proved to have the edge, both the RAF types being armed in the main only with machine guns. The few cannon-armed Spitfires found them in need of further refinement. If the German fighters enjoyed a height advantage and could execute a timely bounce, their cannon proved deadly. Destructive power of cannon shells was invariably greater than that of machine gun rounds – but the liquid-cooled engines powering all three fighters were equally prone to terminal seizure if their cooling systems were hit. As always, it all depended on where and how many rounds struck the target.

In combat with British fighters Bf 109 pilots enjoyed some technical advantage. The Daimler-Benz engines in their Emils were provided with direct fuel injection, whereas the Rolls-Royce Merlins in the Spitfire and Hurricane were fitted with a carburettor system. Under certain flight conditions, negative 'G' could cause the British engine to stop briefly, where the German powerplant carried on. A fix was eventually found by the British, but Werner Mölders, having flown a captured Spitfire in November 1940, was quite scathing in his condemnation of this drawback.

It was not an advantage that the German pilots were able to exploit very often, but they had other advantages. Should they find themselves in real trouble they could always seek altitude since the Bf 109 could operate at a higher ceiling than either of its RAF opponents. Height advantage allowed the Bf 109E to claim numerous kills after high speed dives, preferably from out of the sun. The aim was to catch the British fighters off guard. Tactically, the German 'finger-four' formation was far superior, serving to demonstrate how dated and dangerous were the 'V' formations still generally adhered to by the RAF.

But as the summer of 1940 waned, the *Luftwaffe* was no nearer to beating back the RAF to the point where an invasion force might safely be launched. With the focus of the battle switched to bombing London, increasingly at night, the *Jagdwaffe* was left in something of a vacuum. By the autumn, the stoicism of the German fighter pilots was tested by their first major defeat of the war. Saddled with tactics that were not of their choosing, the *Jagdflieger* made the best of things, but when the bloody business was all but over they were pulled back to rearm and regroup. They were about to

Bf 109E-1s of 8./JG 2 'Richthofen' at an advanced airfield in France in May 1940. Together with the other units of the *Geschwader's* III *Gruppe*, they were soon to be withdrawn to re-equip with the Bf 109E-4.

As this wintry scene shows, the *Jagdwaffe* was not shy when it came to exhibiting its prowess in scoreboards on the ground as well as on aircraft. Taken on a Russian airfield in use by JG 52, the board displays the victories by pilots of *5 Staffel*, backdropped by 'Black 6', a Bf 109F or early G model.

embark on new, even more successful campaigns in the East.

The German fighter force did not terminate the *Kanalkampf* in October 1940. Goering himself insisted on continuing the offensive through nuisance raids, many of which were carried out by Bf 109 fighter-bombers. Each *Staffel* in a *Jagdgeschwader* was ordered to modify their Bf 109s to carry bombs on a belly rack. By flying low, it was found that the raiders could approach the English coast 'under the radar', release their bombs and be away almost before the defences could react. Localised success was often achieved but in essence *Jabo* (*Jagdbomber* or fighter-bomber) operations against England served only to imperil capable fighter pilots in an ultimately pointless campaign of attrition.

During the lull after the *Kanalkampf* the *Jagdwaffe* slowly began to re-equip with the new 'F' model of the Bf 109. To reduce the accident rate suffered by the Emil, Messerschmitt opted to reduce wing loading by removing the weight of the gun mountings and ammunition. He intended to make his fighter lighter and safer to fly by reverting to a battery of one cannon and two machine guns grouped in the fuselage, which remained the standard fixed armament of every subsequent example.

Many pilots thought this lighter armament to be a retrograde step, though the Bf 109F remained deadly in skilled hands. Outwardly much more streamlined than the Emil, its introduction was troubled with the aeroplane suffering a series of disastrous accidents as a result of a weak tail unit. The problem was soon rectified, though not before many pilots had lost faith in the 'F'.

Luftwaffe moves East

The Balkan prelude to Operation *Barbarossa* showed that the *Jagdwaffe's* early victories in Europe could be repeated. Many felt that the failure in the Battle of Britain had been a temporary aberration. The campaigns in Yugoslavia and Greece were the recipe as

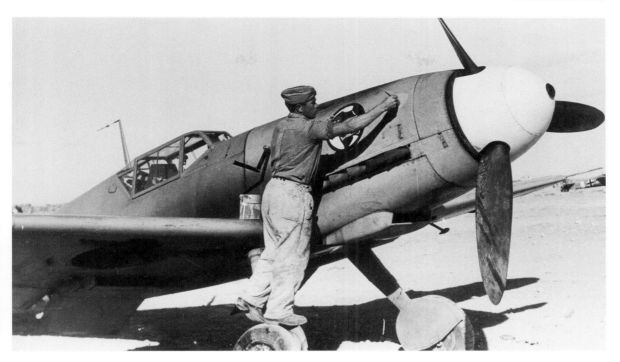

The ultra-clean lines of the Bf 109F are seen to advantage in this view of a machine of JG 27 in North Africa. One of the *Luftwaffe's* problems on the southern front was that many serviceable aircraft had to be abandoned when enemy ground forces overran its airfields. *(BA)*

before – a swift, demoralising ground attack supported by tactical air power with the defending air forces taking high casualties.

Soon afterwards, on 22 June 1941, the massive German attack on the USSR was launched. Fielding 20 *Gruppen* of Bf 109s, the *Luftwaffe* order of battle supported three army groups thrusting into the north to Leningrad, through the centre of the country towards Moscow, and south through the Ukraine and towards the Caucasus oilfields.

The *Jagdwaffe* had a fair idea of the capabilities of the older Russian fighters – after all, the Condor Legion veterans had previously met them over Spain. Bf 109 pilots found little difficulty in breaking up the unwieldy gaggles that the Russians notably adopted in combat. The fighters that equipped the Soviet air force (the VVS or *Voyenno-Vozdushne Sily*) in mid-1941 reflected a similar transitional period that the *Luftwaffe* and other air forces had recently undergone. Defence of the country was partly vested in biplanes such as the Polikarpov I-153,

and the nine year old I-16 monoplane was still a mainstay. However, numbers of the monoplane LaGG-3 were building up dramatically, and the MiG-3 and Yak-1 were entering service.

Russian fighters were largely ineffective in the confusion caused by the German onslaught. During the first six months of *Barbarossa* the *Luftwaffe* fighter force claimed fantastic aerial victory scores. But it was fact not fantasy – a force of just under 800 Bf 109s destroyed as many as 20,000 Soviet aircraft in 1941 and 1942, annihilating the bulk of the pre-war Soviet air force, much of it on the ground.

War over the desert

Just as some of the opposing fighters the *Jagdwaffe* met over Russia would have been familiar, so the pilots of JG 27 again came up against Hurricanes in North Africa. Neither were they overtaxed when intercepting Blenheims, certain combats repeating the success they had had over this same type during the battle for France.

59

It was this kind of terrain that led JG 27 to add extra camouflage to its Bf 109Es in North Africa. It could be very effective, as 'White 3' and 'White 8' demonstrate. A few seconds' delay in seeing his fighter on the part of the enemy was often all a skilled *Jagdflieger* needed to gain the upper hand in combat.

The desert war brought German fliers up against several RAF aircraft that were unique to that theatre, including the Baltimore and Maryland. Other targets included Halifaxes, Bostons and Beaufighters, the latter two demonstrating how the Allies were introducing more capable aircraft as a result of war experience. Continuing to fly the Bf 109E for the time being, the desert *Jagdflieger* only infrequently met these Allied types in combat.

When the first American-supplied fighters were delivered to RAF units in the desert in October 1941, mainly in the shape of the Curtiss P-40 Tomahawk, the small Messerschmitt force still maintained an edge. However, its modest size was a further indication of the limited German commitment to Mussolini's Mediterranean adventure in the face of superior enemy numbers.

Any numerical disadvantage the Germans suffered was offset to a degree by the aircraft of the *Regia Aeronautica*. These included the Macchi C.202 *Veltro*, an excellent fighter comparable to the Bf 109. It was light, manoeuvrable and was powered by a similar DB 601 engine. Its drawbacks also paralleled the Bf 109F, in that its armament of four machine guns was too light to effectively combat the more capable Allied fighter types it increasingly encountered.

During 1942 the improved P-40E Kittyhawk arrived in the Western Desert. Once again this was a fighter that an experienced Bf 109 pilot had little difficulty in getting the better of, if the circumstances were right. The *Jagdflieger* were aided to an extent by RAF tactics and aerial formations that left much to be desired; a defensive circle of Tomahawks was hardly the most aggressive stance and those German pilots who ventured to join in before breaking it up with a few well-aimed bursts could usually pick off several aircraft with ease.

USAAF in the desert

Towards the end of 1942 intelligence reports would have shown the Germans that the British and Commonwealth units ranged against them had been joined by USAAF fighter units equipped not only with P-40s but also with the Bell P-39 Airacobra and the Lockheed P-38

A member of the groundcrew of III./JG 26 seems to be painting on a black wing root stripe to hide the continual staining from the burned oil coming out of the exhaust of a Bf 109F. This was largely a cosmetic feature. *(BA)*

Lightning. There were too few Airacobras deployed to the desert for the *Jagdflieger* to mark up any great success over them, but Bf 109s were well able to take on the P-38Fs flying escort to B-17s and B-24s. By forcing the American pilots to drop below the Lightning's best operating altitude of 15,000 ft (4 572m) the Bf 109s could exploit the big twin-boomed machine's lack of low-speed manoeuvrability. Several American P-38 units suffered a high number of casualties, to the point that the Lockheed fighter was temporarily withdrawn from operations.

History repeated itself when the Spitfire, the Bf 109's most worthy early adversary, arrived in the Western Desert in numbers in 1942. While the less capable Mk V led a new Allied build up, it was followed by Mk VIIIs and IXs, which outperformed the Messerschmitt. By contrast, the improvements incorporated in the comparable Bf 109G were quite limited, and the more effective opposition it faced meant that success often depended on the ability of the pilot to overcome the aircraft's drawbacks rather than to exploit any significant new attributes it had been provided with.

In Europe the *Jagdflieger* found the same creeping disadvantages, not only in the numbers of Allied aircraft but their improved quality. Having since early 1941 intercepted numerous short range probes by Blenheims covered by squadrons first of Hurricanes and then Spitfire Mk Vs, the *Jagdflieger* had usually given as good as they got in a steady war of attrition. The Bf 109F often proved a match for the Spitfire V in straight combat but tactics had to be adapted to offset the disparity in numbers that the 'Channel guard' *Jagdgeschwader* – JG 1, 2 and 26 – often found. When in June 1942 the RAF introduced the Spitfire Mk IX, primarily to counter the Fw 190 rather than the Bf 109, the German pilots saw any edge they had enjoyed being dangerously eroded.

Intercepting RAF anti-shipping aircraft such as the Bristol Beaufort, Westland Whirlwind and Hawker Typhoon brought success to individual Bf 109 pilots, but they were unable to prevent such incursions.

By mid-1943 the RAF was operating Mosquitos, Bostons, Venturas and Mitchells in daylight raids on continental targets while the US 9th Air Force used the excellent B-26 Marauder for the same purpose. All these aircraft could be destroyed by the *Jagdflieger* executing a well-timed bounce – but in the real world that rarely happened. The *Luftwaffe* high command all but ignored the need for mass interception of tactical aircraft attacking targets in the occupied territories.

In a straight comparison with most of its opponents of the mid-war period, the Bf 109 was inferior on some important counts – but that was not something any Allied pilot could rely on. In capable hands the 109 could still hold its own and more. This was particularly true in Russia, where despite its numerical superiority and the progressive introduction of excellent fighters like the Lavochkin La 5 and the Yak 3 and 9, the Red Air Force's casualty figures continued to rise steadily.

Allied intelligence thoroughly examined any new or revised variant of German aircraft as soon as complete examples fell into their hands. This cockpit view shows the first Bf 109F to be captured. Flown by *Hauptmann* Rolf Pingel, a 22 victory ace who was *Kommandeur* of I./JG 53, it was forced down in a controlled belly landing near Dover on 10 July 1941. Salient points include the armour plate back panel to protect the pilot, the Revi gunsight and the prominent port side supercharger air intake.

'Chevron-2,' a Bf 109G-2 of JG 52, displays interesting transitional markings in this photo taken in September 1942. This aircraft was flown by Hans Waldemann, who often acted as wingman to *Gruppenkommandeur* Johannes Steinhoff. The rudder damage was caused by Russian AA fire, which was often very accurate. *(BA)*

The technical gulf was wider in the West, where Bf 109 pilots soon faced further improved Spitfires such as the Griffon-engined Mk XII, the Typhoon, the Tempest and the Mustang III – all of which had gained a definite edge in one way or another.

Also, the numbers game turned relentlessly against the Germans as the Allied aircraft replacement rate rocketed upwards. While enemy fighter numbers were partially matched by output of the Bf 109, the *Luftwaffe* was totally eclipsed in other areas: by late 1943 the *Jagdflieger* could only watch and worry as the quality and quantity of fighters available to their adversaries multiplied.

US long-range fighters

US fighters had already made their presence felt over Germany: the gradual extension of their range had brought the P-47 and P-38 escort fighters right to the threshold of Berlin. In March 1944, Lightnings had appeared above Berlin for the first time. This was unremarkable, in that the P-38 had two engines and was built for range – but when the P-51 Mustang quickly followed, the Germans knew they were in serious trouble. Faster than the Bf 109 and at

least as agile, the P-51 could escort bombers all the way from England and still have enough fuel for a dogfight over the German capital.

Flying from England on a single engine was no mean feat in 1944, and it was one that many, even on the Allied side, had doubted could be done. From that point on the German fighters had to adjust their strategy to take account of escort fighters, preferably by avoiding them before making attacks on the bombers. Separate *Gruppen* of Bf 109s had to be entrusted with countering the escort if the cannon-armed Fw 190s were to get through to the *Viermots*.

After D-Day, the *Wehrmacht's* retreat from France became a debacle, a lesson as to what happens when air cover cannot be provided to ground forces. The German fighter arm tried to provide support on several occasions but was simply overcome by the strength of the opposition, wiped out before it ever reached the areas where it was most needed.

But no matter what the enormity of the setbacks, the Bf 109 *Gruppen* fought on. Only when its airfields were overrun, its fuel exhausted and its pilots incapacitated or dead would the *Jagdwaffe* ever contemplate surrender: few German fighter pilots ever

An eight-man *Luftwaffe* ground crew wheels a Bf 109G-6 (WNr 27083) out for an anti-bomber sortie in the summer of 1944. 'Black 12' must have had a rich running engine, as the black wing root paint, designed to hide the exhaust stains, extends almost out to the wheel well bulges on the wings. *(BA)*

defected to the enemy. To maintain the *Reichvertidigung* (Defence of the Reich) the *Jagdwaffe* relied on its magnificent ground crews who, no matter what disaster had befallen their unit, seemed able to work miracles in preparing enough fighters for each day's missions.

As the Allied tactical air forces closed in on Germany the *Jagdflieger* were just as likely to fall foul of Allied fighter-bombers like the P-47Ds and the P-38s of the 9th Air Force, or the Mustangs and Tempests of the RAF. Success in air combat at any level was now a rare occurrence for the *Luftwaffe*.

Outclassed as it was, the Bf 109G remained the backbone of the fighter arm, far outstripping any other aircraft in terms of production. By mid-1944 the *Luftwaffe* could not risk cutting into output by substituting new types, which might – or might not – have been an improvement over the 109, but which would certainly have disrupted production in the aircraft factories dispersed all over Germany.

Few *Jagdflieger*, heavily involved in day-to-day operations, dwelt at length on any deficiencies in the reliable old *Beule*. They knew they had little choice but to exploit its known combat qualities. And it still had qualities; writing off the Messerschmitt could prove a fatal mistake to an Allied pilot, especially when the Bf 109 was flown by an ace.

Many a US bomber crewman had paid the price of complacency in the past, but by the last winter of the war the escort screen was so strong that the *Jagdflieger* found increasing difficulty in penetrating through to their targets. It still happened, but all too rarely for the German air commanders.

The *Jagdwaffe* absorbed casualties as well as it could, but the losses of fighter pilots who were wounded or killed were not being made good with men of equal calibre. Shortened training periods due to fuel restrictions meant that cadets arriving at combat units were more of a liability than an asset. They required a good

An American GI listens to a discussion which probably concerns the flight characteristics of Bf 109G-10 'Black 10'. The dark coloured band is noteworthy, as are other details including the D/F loop, the flaps and the yellow triangle indicating to the ground crew that only 87 octane rated fuel should be used. *(IWM)*

deal of indoctrination if they were to survive in combat. Additionally, the knowledge that Allied fighters or fighter-bombers could suddenly appear over the training airfield made the process extremely unnerving to instructor and pupil alike.

Not every *Jagdflieger* was the victim of fighters, for the bombers packed a heavy punch that destroyed many a Messerschmitt (though not nearly as many as the American crews claimed). That was hardly surprising, considering that the German pilots, in trying to bring down the most heavily defended bombers in the world, had to press to within a hundred metres to concentrate their cannon and machine gun fire effectively. In this contest, Goliath was beating David hands down.

As Allied troops moved across France, the *Luftwaffe* abandoned many of its forward airfields and was generally pulled back to Germany. There, as in occupied Europe, the fighter *Gruppen* could make use of a network of airfields established with basic servicing and refuelling facilities. This meant that even if the main operational bases were bombed and strafed, precious fighters would not necessarily be lost. Tens of thousands of light, medium and heavy flak guns were deployed on airfield defence. These were very effective in deterring or destroying Allied ground attack aircraft, in the process minimising German pilot casualties and fighter losses.

The Bf 109's war is over

Despite dispersing and camouflaging fighters in bordering woods and therby keeping many of them intact, the *Jagdwaffe* was finally wound down. By late April 1945 the fighter war was over as far as the Bf 109 was concerned. Having boosted the enormous output of Messerschmitt fighters by German companies, hundreds of brand new aircraft were left idle on airfields across eastern Europe as foreign production lines were shut down.

A classic surrender photograph of a Bf 109G-10 which survived the war. The German pilot of 'Black 8' calmly enjoys a smoke while awaiting the arrival of Allied troops on his airfield. In contrast to the aircraft in the previous photo, this one's fuel advisory triangle indicates the use of 84 grade fuel. *(IWM)*

Men of the British 6th Airborne Division examining hangared Bf 109s found at Wunsdorf in April 1945. Each aircraft was awaiting respraying having had its old paintwork rubbed down and the fuselage joints sealed. Three different rudder styles are in evidence. That of the aircraft in the foreground is equipped with two Flettner trim tabs and a more angled lower edge. *(IWM)*

5. Bf 109s Around the World: Versions, Variants and Exports

Bf 109A-0
The Bf 109A designation was retrospectively applied by Messerschmitt AG to identify the first 20 prototype and trials Bf 109s built, including the V3 and the V10. All were powered by the Jumo B, C or D engine; armament was two MG 17 machine guns with no provision for a centreline cannon.

Bf 109B-1
As the first 'mass produced' Bf 109 the B-1 was built by BFW, Erla and Fieseler. Powered by a Jumo 210D driving a two-bladed propeller and armed with three MG 17 machine guns, it was the only version of the Berta model.

Bf 109C-1
The only C series variant to be built; powered by a fuel-injected Jumo 210G engine which drove a two-bladed VDM propeller. Four MG 17 machine guns comprised the armament. A projected C-3 would have had the twin-cannon wing, had this weapon been available.

Bf 109D-1
Fitted with a variable pitch two-bladed VDM propeller, the Bf 109D-1 was powered by a carburettor-equipped Jumo 210D engine and introduced an oil cooler below the port wing.

Bf 109E-0
Revised engine cowling contours to accommodate the DB 601A engine, twin underwing radiators and a braced tailplane served to identify the first of the Emil series, armed with four MG 17 machine guns. The V14 (D-IRIT) served as the prototype and the V15 (D-IPHR) was also converted to E configuration for flight tests.

Bf 109E-1
The first twelve Bf 109E-1s with the DB 601A engine and armament of four machine guns were retained by the parent company on lease-back from the RLM. First flight from Augsburg on 16 November 1938.

Bf 109E-1/B
The suffix indicated a *Bombenanlage* (bomb installation) on the E-1; various racks were fitted (after testing on the V 26) including that for an SD-2 dispenser. Armament was two MG FF cannon and two MG 17 machine guns.

Bf 109E-2
Built in series with the E-3 at Wiener Neustadt (WNF).

Bf 109E-3
Powered by the DB 601A engine the E-3 was the first variant to have MG FF wing cannon as standard and a *Panzerglas* canopy with heavier framing; service from early summer of 1940. Some examples were factory-tropicalised on completion as E-3/trop.

Bf 109E-3a
Export version of the Bf 109E.

Bf 109T-1
Navalised version based on Bf 109E-3 powered by a 1,175 hp DB 601N engine, originally intended for service on carrier *Graf Zeppelin*; wing extended to 36 ft (11.08 m); catapult spools; seven aircraft used for tests, one of which crashed on 3 April 1941.

Bf 109T-2
Extended wing carrier variant converted for land use in 1943. The 109Ts were used operationally by air defence units in Norway.

This nicely refurbished Bf 109E-3 (WNr 4101) is owned by the RAF Museum at Hendon. An ex-II./JG 52 machine, it came down at Manston on 27 November 1940 and is now finished in the markings of an aircraft of I./JG 51. It was given the British serial DG200 during the war, and served with No 1426 (EA) Flight.

Bf 109E-3/B
Fighter bomber version of Bf 109E-3.

Bf 109E-4
Similar to Bf 109E-3 but with additional canopy framing and armoured headrest; MG FF/M wing cannon; 'M' suffix denoted *Minen-Geschosspatrone* (thin-walled charge with self-destruct fuse) rounds which were interspersed with standard ammunition in 60-round drum; first Bf 109 to be tropicalised in numbers.

Bf 109E-4/B
Fighter bomber version of Bf 109E-4.

Bf 109E-4/BN
Similar to E-4 but powered by improved performance, high compression ratio DB 601N engine with maximum rating of 1,175 hp using C 3 (100-octane) fuel.

Bf 109E-5
Tactical reconnaissance version similar to E-1 with DB 601A engine; radio equipment replaced by single Rb 21/18 camera.

Bf 109E-6/N
Tactical reconnaissance version similar to E-1 with DB 601N engine. Two Rb 12.7/7 x 9 cameras fitted between fuselage frames 5 and 6.

Bf 109E-7/B
Extended range fighter bomber able to carry 66-Imp gal (300-ltr) fuel tank or ETC 500 bomb on belly rack.

Bf 109E-7/N
Extended range fighter bomber with revised, high pressure oxygen system.

Bf 109E-7/Z
Extended range fighter bomber with DB 601N engine with GM-1 nitrous oxide boost. Several E-7 variants were given 'U' suffixes when *Umrust-Bausatz*, or factory conversion kits, were applied. Bf 109E-7/U1 covered 208 examples with an armoured radiator; 265 E-7/U2 conversions were fitted with additional armour and SG protected bladder type fuel tanks for close support work. The E-7/U3 had two staggered Rb 12.5/7 x 9 cameras, similar to the Bf 109E-6/N, and was also fitted with the FuG 17 VHF radio.

Bf 109E-8
Extended range fighter powered by DB 601A engine. Based on E-1 but similar fit to the E-7.

Bf 109E-9
Extended range reconnaissance aircraft with Rb 50/30 or Rb 32/7 cameras.

Bf 109F-0
Completely revised airframe with cantilever horizontal stabilizer and rounded wingtips extending span to 32ft 6.5 in (9.92m). Initial examples completed at Regensburg as F series pre-production aircraft with DB 601 engine and engine mounted MG FF/M cannon.

The Bf 109F and early models of the Bf 109G were among the sleekest warplanes of their time, but the tiny size of the airframe meant that it became increasingly difficult to fit new and extra equipment. When larger 13-mm MG 131 heavy machine guns were fitted over the engine in place of the original 7.92-mm MG 17s, the cowling had to be bulged to make room for the bulkier ammunition feed chutes.

Bf 109F-1

Pressurised version externally like Bf 109F-0 which saw service from the autumn of 1940. First example of system of using uneven suffix numbers to denote a pressurised model, but as relatively few such aircraft were actually built, the system fell into disuse.

Bf 109F-2

First major production model of the F series; DB 601N engine with MG 151/15 cannon. Other detail changes compared to early F models; external tail section stiffeners introduced during production after numerous crashes caused by tail failure in earlier 'F' variants. Entered service from January 1941.

Bf 109F-3

Sub-type with DB 601E engine externally similar to F-1 and built from October 1940 to January 1941.

Bf 109F-4

Second major production model of F series for service from June 1941; externally similar to F-2 but with detail changes during production; 20-mm MG 151/20 cannon; Bf 109F-4/R-1 (R suffix denoting *Rustsätze* or field upgrade kits) added two 20 mm MG 151/15 cannon in wing gondolas; many built for reconnaissance role with four different camera installations (Bf-109F-4/R2, /R3, /R4 and /R8); others modified for desert use as Bf 109F-4 trop.

Bf 109F-5

Single example only.

Bf 109G-0

Three pre-production aircraft powered by DB 601E engine pending deliveries of DB 605, October 1941; at least eight more believed completed in early 1942.

Bf 109G-1

Externally similar to F series and G-0 but with DB 605 engine and pressurisation; production completed by July 1942.

Bf 109G-2

Parallel production with G-1 at Regensburg and by Erla between May 1942 and February 1943;

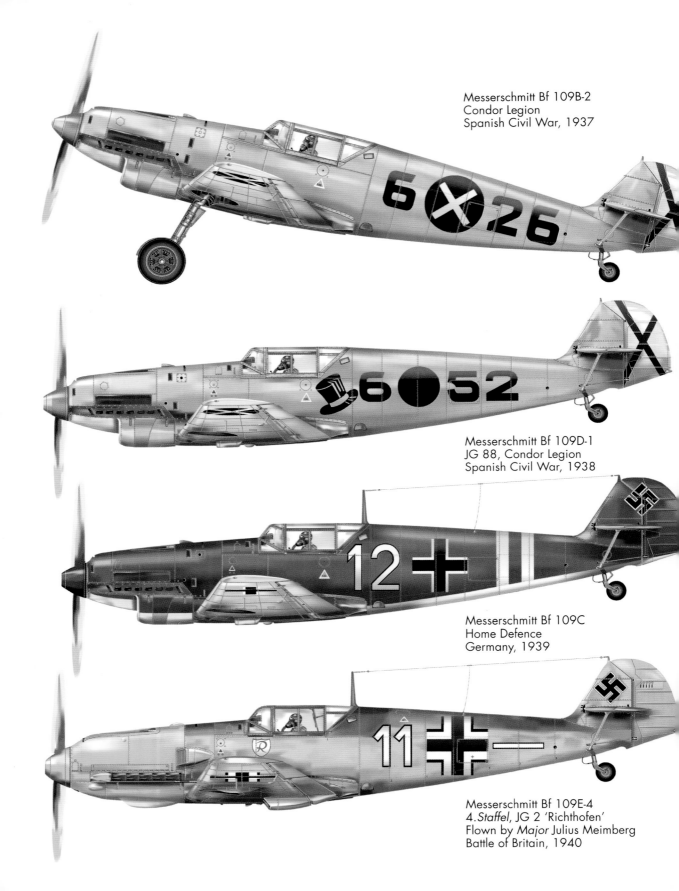

Messerschmitt Bf 109B-2
Condor Legion
Spanish Civil War, 1937

Messerschmitt Bf 109D-1
JG 88, Condor Legion
Spanish Civil War, 1938

Messerschmitt Bf 109C
Home Defence
Germany, 1939

Messerschmitt Bf 109E-4
4.*Staffel*, JG 2 'Richthofen'
Flown by *Major* Julius Meimberg
Battle of Britain, 1940

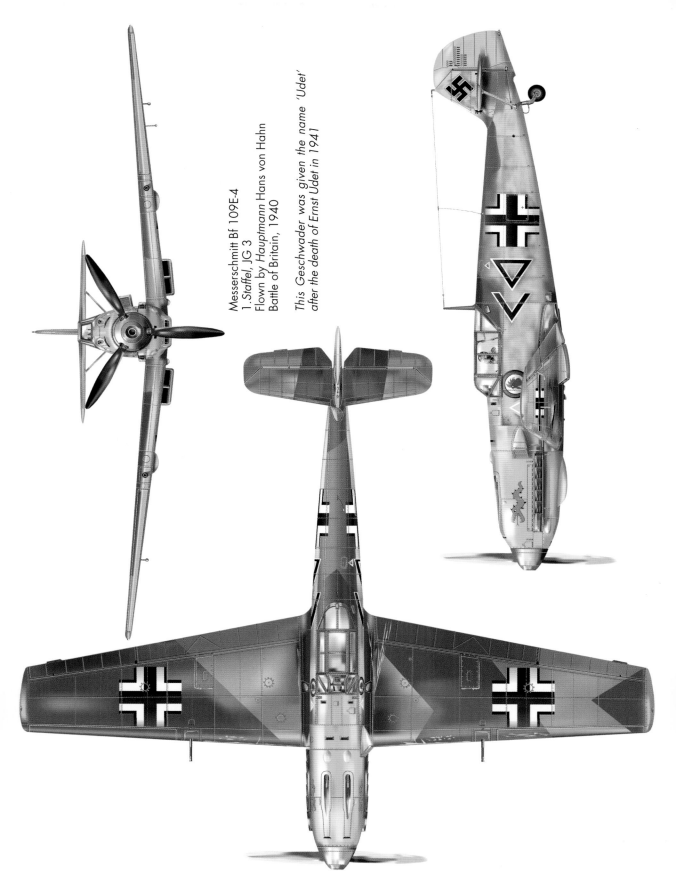

Messerschmitt Bf 109E-4
1.*Staffel*, JG 3
Flown by *Hauptmann* Hans von Hahn
Battle of Britain, 1940

This *Geschwader* was given the name 'Udet'
after the death of Ernst Udet in 1941

Late-model Bf 109Gs and the final Bf 109K variants were virtually identical externally. This is a G-10, upon which the K series was based. It has the 'Galland hood' clear vision canopy fitted to most late 109s, but it lacks the taller tail and longer tailwheel fitted to most examples of the Bf 109K. The G-10 was fitted with a DB-605D engine with MW-50 water-methanol injection that gave it a top speed of 429 mph (690 km/h) at altitude.

one Bf 109Ga-2; *Luftwaffe* service deliveries from June 1942.

Bf 109G-3
Similar to the G-1 but with revised radio equipment; some conversions to two-seat G-12 configuration were undertaken.

Bf 109G-4
Similar to Bf 109G-2 with detail differences; DB 605A engine with GM nitrous oxide boost. Improved service ceiling, to 38,000 ft (11 582 m). Production from October 1942 to July 1943. Three export airframes built as Bf 109Ga-4.

Bf 109G-5
Pressurised version similar to and built in sequence with G-6. Fuselage guns changed to MG 131s.

Bf 109 G-6
Produced in greater numbers than any other Bf 109 variant, the G-6 introduced the distinctive bulges over the spent belt chutes for the MG 131 machine guns, giving rise to the *Beule* or 'Bulge' nickname. The G-6 was the pattern for all subsequent models of the Bf 109. First attempt at standardisation by incorporating all improvements made to that date. The airframe was the basis of numerous re-built examples.

Bf 109G-8
Short range reconnaissance version of the G-6 built by WNF.

Bf 109G-10
Factory conversions of G series aircraft to K-4 standard with new *Werke Nummer*. Fastest of all the Bf 109s, fitted with a DB-605D engine with MW-50 water-methanol injection that gave a speed of 429 mph (690 km/h) at altitude.

Bf 109G-14/AS
Examples powered by the DB 605A engine were interspersed with standard G-6 production.

Bf 109G-12
Two-seat, dual control conversion, first example flew for the first time early in 1944. A fully-instrumented second cockpit was added behind the orginal cockpit, although overall fuselage length was not increased. All examples produced were conversions of existing airframes, primarily earlier G series including G-2s, G-3s, G-4s and G-6s. Mainly used as unarmed conversion, blind flying and instrument trainers, a number of G-12s retained armament to fulfill a gunnery training role.

Bf 109G-14
The most numerous Bf 109 variant issued to operational units from mid-1944 until the end of the war. As an attempt to standardise the Bf 109 by incorporating all the improvements introduced on the G-6, the G-14 failed, since scores of variations appeared.

The *Erla-Haube*, seen here fitted to Hans Dittes' Bf 109G, was the nearest the Germans got to a clear-view canopy for the aircraft. Often known as the 'Galland hood', this one incorporates the transparent section in the armour plate designed both to protect the pilot's head and enable him to see behind. *(BJMarsh)*

Powered by the DB 605AM/AS engine with MW-50 injection, the aircraft was completed with either short or tall tail design, the rudder being fitted with one or two Flettner trim tabs, but the *Erla-Haube* and *Peilrufanlage* were standard. From late 1944 the larger 660 x 190-mm mainwheels required new rectangular upper wing fairings to fully enclose them. The wing conversion was seen on only a small number of G-14s as well as some G-6s and G-8s.

Bf 109G-14/AS
The equivalent of the Bf 109G-6/AS, this version, of which about 1,000 were built, was intended to have the Fo 987 oil cooler, but many retained the shallower Fo 870 type.

Bf 109K-3
Intended interim pressurised Bf 109K variant with DB 605ASD engine with GM-1 boost but only one example built. Variant cancelled in favour of the K-4.

Bf 109K-4
Last of the wartime line, the Bf 109K-4 was powered by the DB 605D engine and the only one of the *Kurfurst* series to actually enter *Luftwaffe* service and see action. Deliveries commenced in October 1944 and continued until the last weeks of the war. Another attempt at standardisation, the K-4 invariably featured a tall vertical tailplane with either of the rudder tab arrangements and Erla hood. Some aircraft also had the DB 605AS engine, so the *Werke Nummer* remains the most reliable guide to identity.

Stillborn variants
Bf 109H
Of all the projected variants of the Bf 109, that built for an ultra high-altitude role would have been most able to exploit the type's proven capability in this respect, by incorporating an

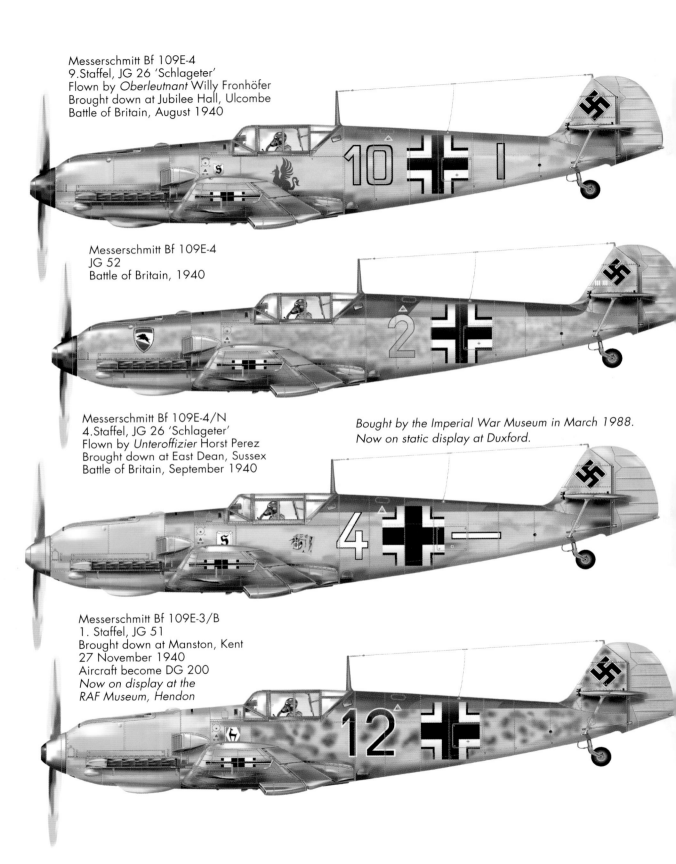

Messerschmitt Bf 109E-4
9.Staffel, JG 26 'Schlageter'
Flown by *Oberleutnant* Willy Fronhöfer
Brought down at Jubilee Hall, Ulcombe
Battle of Britain, August 1940

Messerschmitt Bf 109E-4
JG 52
Battle of Britain, 1940

Messerschmitt Bf 109E-4/N
4.Staffel, JG 26 'Schlageter'
Flown by *Unteroffizier* Horst Perez
Brought down at East Dean, Sussex
Battle of Britain, September 1940

Bought by the Imperial War Museum in March 1988.
Now on static display at Duxford.

Messerschmitt Bf 109E-3/B
1. Staffel, JG 51
Brought down at Manston, Kent
27 November 1940
Aircraft become DG 200
Now on display at the
RAF Museum, Hendon

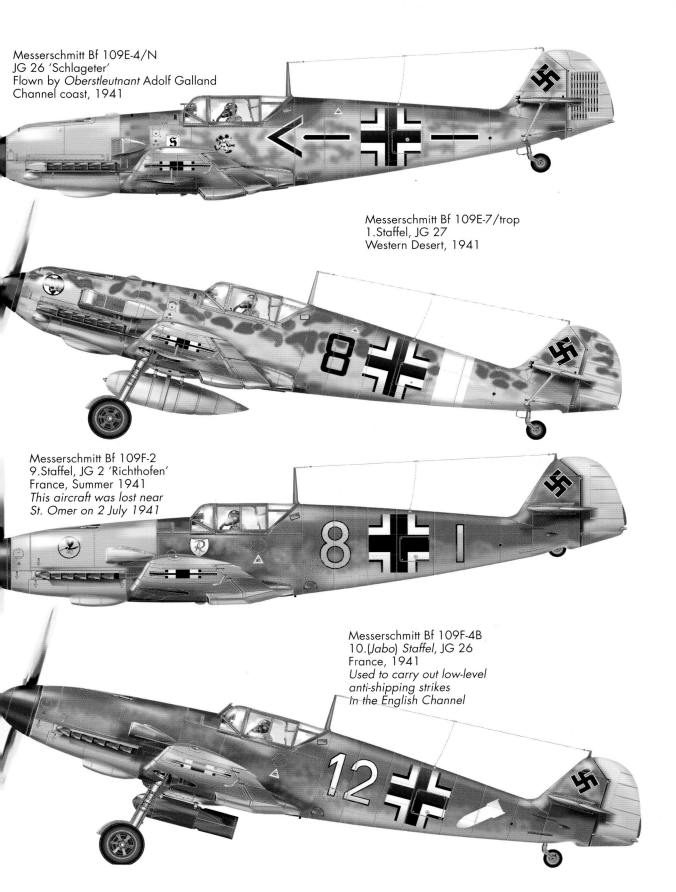

Messerschmitt Bf 109E-4/N
JG 26 'Schlageter'
Flown by *Oberstleutnant* Adolf Galland
Channel coast, 1941

Messerschmitt Bf 109E-7/trop
1.Staffel, JG 27
Western Desert, 1941

Messerschmitt Bf 109F-2
9.Staffel, JG 2 'Richthofen'
France, Summer 1941
*This aircraft was lost near
St. Omer on 2 July 1941*

Messerschmitt Bf 109F-4B
10.(*Jabo*) *Staffel*, JG 26
France, 1941
*Used to carry out low-level
anti-shipping strikes
in the English Channel*

extended wing. Flown and tested in 1943 as a single converted F model, the Bf 109 H-0 was powered by a DB 601E-1 engine with GM 1 boost and had a 6ft 6.6in (2m) wing extension and a braced tailplane.

The Bf 109H series looked promising enough to be included in the *Luftwaffe's* final order of battle projections for late 1945/46 – and indeed would probably have been the last Bf 109 variant to see service – but in the event the new sub-type lost out to the extended span Ta 152H. Comparing the published altitude figures for both aircraft the Bf 109H-1 was credited with a ceiling of 47,890 ft (14 596 m) while the Ta 152H could attain 48,560 ft (14 800 m).

Under evaluation as the Germans surrendered were the potentially excellent Bf 109K-6, K-8, K-10 and K-14 variants, developed models that might have entered service had the war lasted. The Bf 109K-6 had reached an advanced stage of evolution some time beforehand but problems with airframe construction and engine supply were enough to prevent any production being initiated.

The ultimate Bf 109K, disregarding more advanced 'paper projects', was to have been the K-14 with the DB 605L engine incorporating an improved two-stage mechanical supercharger giving 1,700 hp for take off. A four-bladed airscrew similar to that planned for the Bf 109H series was to be fitted, as were wooden wings supplied by the Wolf Firth concern. Most importantly, this model would have finally reinstated a pair of integral wing cannon that the aircraft had lacked for so long. A third centreline MK 108 cannon and two MG 151 machine guns completed a formidable armament package.

The first runs of the DB 605 L were made in 1944 but the engine was not expected to be available until the following year.

The manufacture of wooden airframe components, ostensibly more economical than aluminium, was beset with insurmountable problems in the chaotic dying weeks of the Third Reich. Firth experienced enough

On the port side of the DB 605, the large size and shape of the supercharger shows why the exterior of the cowling had to be modified to fit over the breeches of the twin machine guns mounted above it. The smaller of the two containers holds oil, the lower one being the glycol header tank. *(Marsh)*

The last evolved version of the Bf 109 was the "Me 209-II", which had nothing to do with the pre-war Me 209 racer. The Me 209-II had a redesigned tail; landing gear that hinged in the wings instead of the fuselage, eliminating the Bf 109's troublesome narrow track; uprated engine; a taller vertical tailplane; and a DB-603 engine with an annular radiator that misleadingly suggested a radial engine. By late spring 1944 all work on the Me 209 had been abandoned, as compatibility with existing production lines had almost completely evaporated.

difficulties in moulding the complex shape of the undercarriage wells and achieving a firm wood to metal bond for OKL to seriously doubt its viability and cancellation followed.

In the event all Bf 109K derivatives would probably have been cancelled, in line with a stated intention for the *Jagdwaffe* to become almost entirely a turbojet fighter force as soon as possible. Initially, however, by mid to late 1945, units previously flying the Bf 109G were to receive the K-4, primarily to reduce the uneconomical stockpiling of components required for a variety of different versions. Plans for German fighter deployment projected forward to March 1946 envisaged the phase-out of all Bf 109s apart from the high altitude H-2 model.

Projects

In common with almost every other German production aircraft, Messerschmitt projected the basic airframe into a number of ideas that generally remained firmly on the drawing board. These were often paper exercises that had decreasing chances of being built as Germany's military position worsened. One of those intended to increase the range of the Bf

109 was the so-called Bf 109Z (*Zwilling* or twin) which would have been created by joining two F series fuselages with common wing and tailplane sections. The starboard cockpit area was to be blanked off, the pilot flying the aircraft from the port fuselage.

Numerically the Bf 109 series extended to take in the various Me 209s and 309s built (and in some cases flown) during the war, as well as the planned 409, 509 and finally the Me 609.

Intended originally as a sucessor to the Bf 109, three Me 309 V-series aircraft were flown and two of these joined together, much like the Bf 109Z, would have created the Me 609. Mention should also be made of the Bf 109TL which was a twin turbojet project based around the Me 155, a radically different aircraft despite utilising many Bf 109 components and which was contracted out to Blohm und Voss.

Postwar variants
Avia S 199

Leonard 'Kit' Carson, the US fighter ace who frequently met the Bf 109 in combat and was in a position to know what he was talking about, penned a fascinating 'check list' of what Willy Messerschmitt might have done to improve the

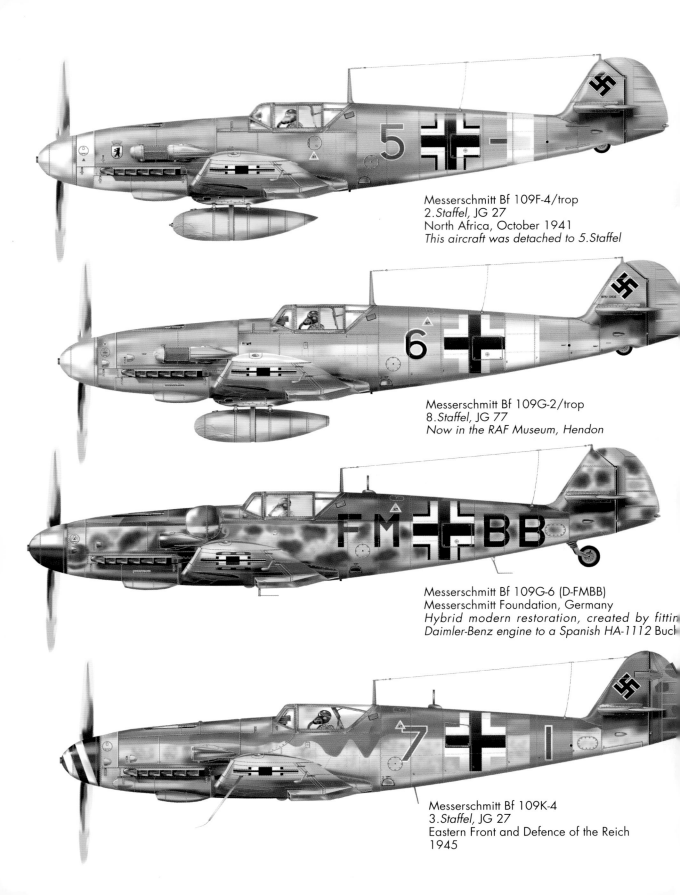

Messerschmitt Bf 109F-4/trop
2.*Staffel*, JG 27
North Africa, October 1941
This aircraft was detached to 5.Staffel

Messerschmitt Bf 109G-2/trop
8.*Staffel*, JG 77
Now in the RAF Museum, Hendon

Messerschmitt Bf 109G-6 (D-FMBB)
Messerschmitt Foundation, Germany
*Hybrid modern restoration, created by fittin
Daimler-Benz engine to a Spanish HA-1112 Buch*

Messerschmitt Bf 109K-4
3.*Staffel*, JG 27
Eastern Front and Defence of the Reich
1945

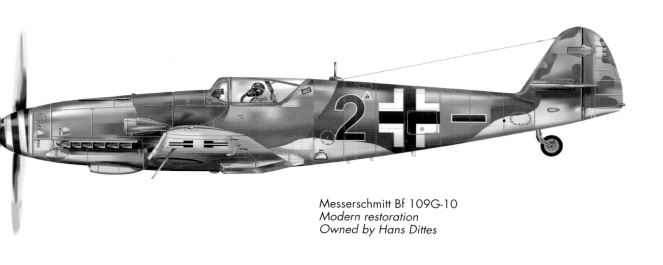

Messerschmitt Bf 109G-10
Modern restoration
Owned by Hans Dittes

Messerschmitt Bf 109E-3/B
Repaired after wheels-up landing in Kent, 1940
Used extensively for evaluation by the RAF

Messerschmitt Bf 109E-3
Swiss *Fliegertruppe*
1940

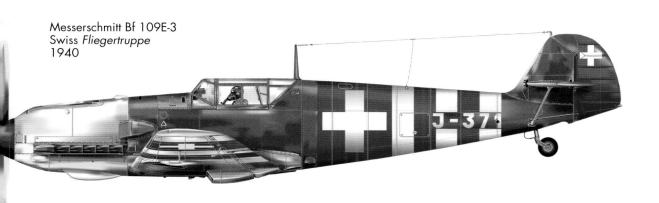

The Swiss, the first export customer for the Bf 109, acquired Bf 109Gs in exchange for an Me 110G night fighter which landed in Switzerland by mistake. The Germans agreed to sell ten Bf 109Gs provided the night fighter and its highly secret avionics was safely returned or was destroyed. The deal went through but the Swiss, chagrined at the poor condition of their Gustavs, demanded compensation for the cost of making them operational. This aircraft (WNr 163245) was damaged beyond repair on 13 November 1946. *(MAP)*

Bf 109. Among Carson's suggestions were: remove the camouflage paint and thereby save about 50 pounds (22 kg) in weight; change the cockpit canopy to that of the Me 209 V1; lock shut the wing slats, thereby eliminating the tubulence they created and at the same time put in two degrees of wing 'washout'; modify the coolant air scoops to reduce drag; retract the tailwheel and completely enclose it by doors.

Only the last of these improvements was carried out and then only partially. Ironically it was the Czech Avia company which did incorporate some of these modifications, including the fitting of a much more convenient sliding, clear view cockpit canopy on the postwar S 199 which was powered by the Jumo 211F engine.

With the war over Avia decided to continue producing the Bf 109G-14 to equip a postwar Czech Air Force. Little changed from standard German machines, these early peacetime Gustavs were fitted with the DB 605 engine until a fire destroyed most of the stocks. Company engineers then partially redesigned the Bf 109G airframe to take the Jumo 211 powerplant and turn it into the S 199.

Unfortunately the S 199, known as the *Mezec* or 'Mule', was widely reckoned to be the worst handling '109 of them all due to the high torque of the engine, which had been designed for installation in a twin-engined bomber. Avia built 422 S 199s between 1946 and 1949 with Letov adding 129 to bring the total to 551. To aid pilot conversion a number of two-seaters were produced as the CS-199.

Subsequently the Israeli Air Force acquired 25 examples of the Mule (all appearing to have the wartime *Erla-Haube* rather than the Czech clear view hood) to bolster its desperate fight against its Arab neighbours. Adding to the irony of Jewish pilots flying a German-derived aircraft was the fact that the Israeli Air Force briefly saw combat with Royal Egyptian Air Force Spitfires, bringing the Bf 109's combat career full circle.

The Middle Eastern conflict is believed to have been the last occasion when a fighter based on Willy Messerschmitt's 1934 design fired its guns in anger at its old adversary. The clash took place over Gaza on 16 October 1948, eight years and some seven months since the Bf 109E first engaged Spitfires over the French

After the war Avia continued to build Bf 109s, but when the Czechs lost their stock of DB engines in a fire they mated the Junkers Jumo 211 to the Bf-109G airframe, resulting in the Avia S-199. Unfortunately, the Jumo was optimised for low RPM and high torque, and the S-199 was a nightmare to fly. Czech pilots gave it the contemptuous nickname of *Mezec* or 'Mule'. This is a two-seat conversion trainer variant, the CS-199.

coast on 23 May 1940. Both engagements ended with the demise of a Spitfire. At the controls of the Avia S 199 marked with the blue star of David was Rudy Augarten of No 101 Sqn, who claimed one Egyptian Spitfire.

That was not quite the end of the Bf 109's operational story however, as the aircraft continued to serve the Swiss Air Force after the end of WWII. Having been the earliest pre-war customer for the aircraft the *Flugwaffe* continued to operate the type in defence of Swiss neutrality until 28 December 1949 when the surviving Bf 109s were withdrawn.

Export 109s

Before the war the Bf 109 was sold to a number of countries, and notwithstanding the sole Swiss order for Bf 109D-1s, the Bf 109E-3 model (for export purposes known as the Bf 109E-3a) was the version supplied in the most substantial numbers. During the hostilities after 1939 Germany's Axis partners were supplied with varying quantities of Bf 109s in a number of different variants.

Bulgaria

Deliveries of the Bf 109E, the aircraft the *Vozdushni Voiski* (Royal Bulgarian Air Force) named the 'Arrow,' began during 1940-41 with

19 examples of the Bf 109E-3as and continued with the E-4 and E-7 to total 69. At least five examples of the Bf 109F-2 and F-4 were also supplied but the largest numbers were reserved for the Bf 109G-2, G-4, G-6 and G-10, totalling at least 145 although one source puts the figure for Gustav deliveries at 'more than 200'.

On 10 October 1941 the 682nd and 692nd Squadrons of the 6th Fighter Regiment formed with Bf 109Es. These were flown on the Eastern Front until the spring of 1943, when 16 Bf 109G-2s were delivered, followed by 13 more that summer. The number of Bulgarian-operated Gustavs had risen to 48 by August 1943, with further aircraft being supplied by early 1944. The above figure of 145 Bf 109Gs was certainly on hand by 1 May 1944 and many of these aircraft survived the war to be passed on to Yugoslavia.

Croatia

Pilots of the Croatian Legion's 4th Air Force Group with its 10th and 11th Fighter *Jato* (squadrons) were attached to the *Luftwaffe* for combat in the East from October 1941. Constituting 15.*(kroat)*/JG 52, they flew German-owned Bf 109Es and Fs. The 10th *Jato* saw action first and was joined by the 11th in December, but the latter was disbanded due to a lack of aircraft and was absorbed by the 10th. In July 1942 seven Bf 109G-2s arrived, followed by enough to fully equip the unit. Known variously as the 'Dzal fighter group' after its CO, Major Franjo Dzal, or the Ustasha Legion on account of the badge displayed prominently under the cockpit of its Bf 109s, the 10th gained a reputation for prowess in battle. At the same time it suffered an accelerated rate of defections to the Soviet side which brought about a second grounding order in March 1944 following one enforced by the Germans in July 1943.

Returning to combat in June 1944 as the 1. *kroatische Jagdstaffel* under *Luftflotte* 6, the unit finally received Bf 109G-10s and G-14s but more defections led the Germans to ground it for a third time – and bring to an end Croat service on the Eastern Front. The pilots then found themselves participating in the bloody civil war against communist partisans at home and defending its airspace against Allied air raids. Tito's hold on the area was such that there was nothing a handful of Bf 109 pilots could do to stave off the inevitable, and more defections in 1945, this time to the Western Allies, all but ended the Croat Air Force.

Finland

While she was allied to Germany, Finland was supplied with a total of 162 Bf 109s. The first transfer of 30 Bf 109G-2s, enough to form a new fighter squadron (*HLeLv* 34) took place in March 1943. The unit saw combat during the 1942-44 Continuation War and any attrition among these Bf 109s was made good by replacements. Flying against the Soviets during their 1944 offensive, Finland purchased an additional 112 Bf 109G-6s and two G-8s, enough to equip *HLeLv* 24 and part of *HLeLv* 30. Some Bf 109 combat missions were flown against the Germans following the armistice signed with Russia on 19 September 1944.

Hungary

Hungary's declaration of war on the Soviet Union on 27 June 1941 made her Germany's ally and eligible for military assistance. Two Bf 109Ds were delivered to the *Magyar Kiralyi Honved Legiero* (Royal Hungarian Air Force) in 1941, followed by 66 Bf 109E-4/Bs, 84 G-2s and G-4s and a further 50 Bf 109E-4s.

The Hungarians were attached to JG 52, where they formed 1.*Ungarische Jabostaffel* (1st Hungarian Fighter-Bomber Squadron) with Bf 109F-4s. Fighter Squadrons 1/1, 2/1 and 5/3 which became 101/2, 101/1 and 101/3 respectively, all flew Bf 109s on home defence. After going through a number of designation changes the 101st Fighter Wing, the famed 'Red Pumas,' scored a string of victories over the USAAF before the war moved on. Fighting hard to keep the Red Army from taking Budapest and supporting a doomed final German counter offensive aimed at securing the city, the Bf 109 regiment pulled back into Austria and finally had to admit defeat in May 1945. Personnel set fire to their aircraft and the MKHL ceased to exist.

Having completed its first Bf 109Ga-4 on 21 December 1942 the Gyor plant delivered 205 Bf 109G-2s, G-4s and G-6s in 1943 and later added 33 G-10s and G-14s. Local production thus raised the total number of Bf 109s in Hungarian service to 440, although one source puts this higher, at 471.

Italy

Germany supplied the *Regia Aeronautica* with enough Bf 109s to equip two *Gruppi*, No.3 (153, 154 and 155 *Squadriglia*) and No.150 (363, 364 and 365 *Squadriglia*), mainly to defend Sicily and Italy during 1943. The total number of aircraft passed to the RA has been quoted as approximately 15 F-4s, six G-2s, ten G-4s and 91 G-6s, a total of at least 122.

When Badoglio ousted Mussolini and signed an armistice with the Allies on 8 September 1943, the pro-Fascist *Aeronautica Nazionale Repubblicana* (ANR) was formed by the rump fascist government in the north, and the Bf 109G equipped two units. The first 43 examples were Bf 109G-6/R-6s formerly on the strength of I./JG 53 and II./JG 77, which arrived in May 1944. No.2. *Gruppo* flew its first operational sorties on 22 June 1944, suffering heavy losses in air combat and destruction on the ground. It was joined by No 1 *Gruppo*, and a third group was about to enter combat when hostilities ceased. All known ANR-operated Bf 109s were Gustavs (G-6, G-10 and G-14) and at least 100 are believed to have been transferred.

The Finns flew 162 Bf-109s, scoring 270 kills for the loss of 22 up to the time of the armistice with the Soviets in September 1944. Finnish ace Eino Juutilainen scored 94 victories, making him (with the possible exceptions of Hiroyoshi Nishizawa and Tetsuzo Iwamoto of Japan) the highest-scoring non-German fighter pilot in history.

Japan

Ten examples of the Bf 109E-3a were shipped to Japan in 1940 for evaluation preceding possible licence production and combat use by the Japanese Army Air Force. Three more E models followed in 1941 and even though the type never entered service, the Allies saw fit to allocate the reporting codename 'Mike,' just in case Japanese Bf 109s were ever encountered by Allied airmen in the Pacific war.

Rumania

Eleven Bf 109E-3as were delivered to Rumania in 1940, with 39 ex-*Luftwaffe* training aircraft being despatched in 1941 and 15 in 1942. Germany transferred five F-2s and F-4s plus approximately 200 G-2s, G-4s and G-6s, a total that perhaps reflects the esteem in which the Rumanians were held by Germany. A single G-12 trainer and another 48 G-2s were also transferred. The *Industria Aeronautica Romana* (I.A.R.) plant at Brasov tooled up to build the Bf 109G-4 and G-6 (as the Ga-4 and Ga-6

respectively) and despite the late start-up date of April 1944, the plant managed to deliver 75 Gustavs before the Russians invaded and forced Rumania to break with the Axis in August 1944. Up to that point about 349 Bf 109s had entered service.

Slovakia

With the German takeover of the country in 1939, the Czechoslovakian Air Force ceased to exist. Bohemia and Moravia became German protectorates, while a puppet state was set up in Slovakia. The Germans utilised the efficient pre-war aircraft industry to build trainers, before switching to the Bf 109G-14. Avia established a Messerschmitt production line at Prague in 1945 but only 15 aircraft were apparently completed before the war's end.

The Slovak Air Force was eligible for re-equipment by Germany, and pilot training on the Bf 109E commenced during 1942. The following year 43 Bf 109s were transferred to Slovak control, these being F-2s, F-4s, G-2s and

Decked out as Emils for the film "Battle of Britain", a good part of the Spanish Air Force's surplus stock of HA-1112 *Buchons* was seen at locations in the UK and Europe for the take off and aerial sequences of the film.

Marginally more authentic in appearance when fitted with a three rather than four bladed prop, this *Buchon* owner appears to have mixed variants by fitting simulated wing cannon. The pot-bellied look of the Spanish aircraft has driven some owners to fit a genuine Daimler-Benz engine – but genuine DBs can be hard to find, and the conversion job can also be frustratingly difficult. *(RAF Shawbury)*

Bf 109G-2 'Black 6' on the Imperial War Museum's Duxford flight line. The magnificent restoration attracted many 'repeat visits' from people associated with the aircraft during the war, including the Germans who had flown it in North Africa and the Australians who first put the aircraft on the road to preservation – although they were obviously not aware of that at the time they captured it. *(B J Marsh)*

G-4s. In March enough G-6s were loaned to equip 13./(slow)JG 52 for service in the East, and this unit flew combat missions until being withdrawn from Russia at the end of the year. A Slovakian 12th Fighter Squadron was also formed with loaned Bf 109G-6s.

Originally operating old Bf 109Es, replaced by 14 G-6s, the 13th Fighter Squadron defended Bratislava and lost heavily to USAAF fighters. By the time of the communist Slovak uprising on 29 August 1944, the 12th and 13th Squadrons were almost out of aircraft and the overthrow of the revolt spelt the end of the Slovak Air Force.

Spain

Apart from the 44 Bf 109E-3a supplied to Spain in 1939 at the end of the civil war, several examples of the Bf 109 *Versuchs* machines plus numerous Bf 109As, Bs, Cs and Ds were left behind when the Condor Legion departed. During World War II, Spain formed a foreign legion known as the *Escuadrion Azul* (Blue Division), the air element of which formed five *escadrilles* which were attached to German *Jagdgeschwadern* operating on the Eastern Front.

Germany supplied enough Bf 109E-7s to equip the initial unit, 1a *Escadrille* which became 15.(span)/JG 27 in 1941.

The other Spanish volunteer units were equipped with the Bf 109F-4, and each took its place in the front line, successively becoming 15.(span)/JG 51. The 4th *Escadrille* later re-equipped with the Fw 190A and the 5th was given the Bf 109G-6 which it used until Franco pulled the Blue Division out of Russia – much to the disgust of his fighter pilots – in 1943. In total these five Spanish units claimed 159 Soviet aircraft downed, for the loss of 21 pilots killed, wounded or made PoW.

In 1943 25 Bf 109G-2s arrived in Spain without engines and other items. Hispano Aviacion obtained a manufacturing licence, initially to complete these airframes by installing the 1,300 hp Hispano-Suiza HS-12-Z-89. A test fitting in one of the stored G-2s brought about the designation HA-1109-J1L under which the remaining G-2s were completed. One flew with an HS-12-Z-17 engine also of 1,300 hp and was known as an HA-1109-K1L. A further example was modified as a two-seat trainer as an HA-1110-K1L.

85

The distinctive engine cowling contours of the late-production Bf 109s are well captured in this view of German owner Hans Dittes' G-10 at Duxford before its return to its present home in Germany. *(Marsh)*

After the war, ironically, Spanish Bf 109s were fitted with Merlin engines built under licence from Rolls-Royce. The revised nose contours created by the engine which had powered the 109's greatest foes spawned the name *Buchon*, which means 'fat pigeon'.

Switzerland

The only country to purchase the Bf 109D-1 directly, Switzerland took delivery of 10 examples which served between 1939 and 1949. This was followed by further orders for 80 Bf 109E-3a models, delivered in two batches of 56 and 24 in 1939 and 1940 respectively. Two Bf 109Fs were acquired in 1942 and in May 1944 14 G-6s were delivered in return for the destruction of a Bf 110G night fighter – and its highly secret electronic equipment – that had landed in error on Swiss soil.

USSR

Three examples of the Bf 109E-3a were purchased by the USSR before the war. After June 1941 the Red Air Force captured a substantial number of Bf 109s of all models. The air element of the ill-fated anti-Stalin *Russkaya Osvoboditelnaya Armiya* (ROA) or Russian Liberation Army, which was raised to fight alongside the Germans, was equipped with Bf 109s. Politics, however, prevented Russian

pilots from mounting more than one effective combat operation. ROA Fighter Squadron 5 'Kazakov' was equipped with 16 Bf 109G-10s in March 1945, but saw no serious action.

Yugoslavia

In 1939 and 40 Germany supplied 73 Bf 109E-3a models to the *Jugoslovensko Kraljevsko Ratno Vazduhoplovstvo* (JKRV), and 61 remained in service when the Germans invaded. By the time of the Yugoslav surrender on 17 April 1941, most had been destroyed in combat or burnt to prevent their capture.

When Yugoslav pilots were in a position to support the partisan People's Liberation Army during 1944, the *Eskadrila za vezu* was issued with about ten Bf 109G-6s and G-10s, mostly captured Croatian Air Force aircraft. They flew their final mission on 28 May 1945 when a single Ju 87 escorted by Bf 109G-10s bombed German troops who refused to surrender.

After the war, 17 Bf 109Gs were based at Zagreb and Beograd airfields but these were not flown until 1947 when 59 more G-2s, G-10s and G-12s were received from Bulgaria to form the 83rd Fighter Wing, *Jugoslavensko Ratno Vazduhoplovstvo* (JRV) at Cerklje. Several were passed to the 172nd Wing which shared the base. Flown extensively on defensive patrols, the Gustavs were not retired until mid-1952.

Appendix 1
Bf 109 Weapons

Guns

One of several World War II fighters designed to accommodate a cannon utilising a blast tube between the engine cylinder blocks, the Bf 109 was for some years actually armed only with a pair of Rheinmetall-Borsig MG 17 machine guns of 7.92-mm calibre, set into troughs in the upper forward fuselage decking. Firing at a rate of 1,100 rounds per minute (rpm) these guns had a short recoil action, fed by a disintegrating link belt. The centreline cannon was not fitted as standard until the appearance of the Bf 109F late in 1940. The reason was that the barrel of the Oerlikon FFS (on which the MG/FF, Germany's standard 20-mm weapon of the time was based) was actually too large to fit the 70-mm bore between the DB cylinder blocks.

To improve the Bf 109E's firepower in lieu of a cannon, a 'gun wing' was developed to house a second pair of MG 17 machine guns in the leading edge. Although reports from Spain confirmed that even four machine guns were inadequate, little could be done to increase it until the wing guns could be changed to 20-mm cannon. Consequently the Bf 109B, C and D series carried up to four rifle-calibre MG 17s, which did at least result in an improved spread of fire.

The Bf 109E carried two 20-mm MG/FF cannon in the wings, each fed by a 60-round drum magazine. This required a bulged fairing under each wing panel, reloading being achieved from beneath. Operating on the blowback principle, the cannon operated at a cyclic rate of 520 rpm.

When Messerschmitt set about designing an improved Bf 109 rather than build on the armament of the E series, he abandoned integral wing cannon for the Bf 109F and opted instead for a fuselage-only grouping, with the new MG 151 20-mm cannon being fitted into the existing engine mount. This met with considerable criticism from some pilots, who thought the reduction in firepower to be a retrograde step. Pitted against increasingly well protected and armed enemy

Twin cowling mounted machine guns were once the sole armament of the Bf 109. Of various different calibres during the aircraft's long production life, they supplemented the cannon on those aircraft where the latter weapon was fitted. (Marsh)

Access to the Bf 109G's centreline cannon was rather constrained, although the system of feeding the shells into guides via the wing hatch appeared to give little trouble. A painted cockerel's head visible just above the neck of the man on the left identifies the unit as III./JG 2. (BA)

aircraft, the Bf 109F was sometimes hard put to inflict enough damage to bring them down. But from the point of view of the *Experten*, who were almost invariable superbly accurate shots and were more capable at deflection shooting, the Bf 109F was very much a pilot's aeroplane.

The 7.92-mm weapons in the nose were easy to service, and were set close enough to the cannon to give a concentrated cone of fire. Each MG 17 was provided with 500 rounds, the MG 151 with 200. Cannon ammunition was stored in a box inside the port wing root, the belt being feed through wing access hatches into guides and attached via the quick release breech cover in the cockpit. Spent cartridges and links from all three weapons were collected in two trays in the fuselage underside.

Underwing cannon

Any deficiency in firepower was partially met by gondola fairings which enclosed the breech of a 20-mm cannon; these MG 151/20 or MG/FF cannon gondolas were ready for service during the production run of the Bf 109F and were tested on the F-4. Little use was made of them until the advent of Allied heavy bomber raids in 1943. Pilots had some reservations about using these weapons which, although effective, increased drag. The MG 151/20 was a short recoil weapon fed by a disintegrating link belt and operated electrically at a cyclic firing rate of 800 rpm.

Each gondola, shaped slightly differently depending on which cannon it enclosed, was factory-fitted and attached to a wing mounting plate riveted on as a 'self-contained' unit immediately outboard of the landing gear legs. The magazine and ammunition tracks were integral with the gun mounting and links and spent rounds were ejected from a slot in the side of the gondola, which hinged downwards for servicing. The entire cannon could be removed without need to detach the wing panel. Aircraft so fitted were known colloquially as *Kannonboot* (gunboat) Messerschmitts, though the official *Rustsätze* designation on the Bf 109G-6 and subsequent variants was R6. A third cannon gondola was test fitted experimentally below the centre fuselage, about where the wiring for an ETC bomb rack was located, but this was apparently never used operationally on the Bf 109.

Testing of the much more powerful 30-mm Rheinmetall MK 108 cannon began in the summer of 1942. This weapon fired a powerful, 330g projectile which could destroy a four-engined bomber with four or five hits, but it had a low muzzle velocity – which translated into an insufficiently flat trajectory – and a relatively slow firing rate (hence the nickname 'pneumatic hammer') of 600/650 rpm. The disintegrating link belt held 60 rounds.

Gunsights

Throughout its long service life, the Bf 109 relied on a series of excellent reflector gunsights produced by the Zeiss-Revi company. Bf 109Es were fitted with the C/12/C or C/12/D sight, which was progressively updated, the Revi 16 B being fitted into the Bf 109G-5 and G-6, for example. A modification adopted by Adolf Galland was a sight enhancer, which did not prove to have much advantage in combat.

Most effective against 'soft' ground targets, the four 50 kg bombs on an ETC centreline rack were quite frequently used by Bf 109 Gruppen. Shackling them in the freezing wastes of a Russian winter was not however the most envied of ground crew tasks. (BA)

Armour

Pilot armour was first fitted to the Bf 109E-3 and E-4. By the time the Bf 109G entered service, pilot protection consisted of a 10-mm angled plate to protect the pilot's head and two backplates, one of 8-mm thickness the other of 24-mm. The bullet proof glass shield, set at an angle of about 60 degrees, was 63-mm thick.

Rockets

Pending any significant uprating of its guns, the Bf 109G-6 was adapted to carry a pair of 210-mm rockets in underwing launching tubes. They were issued in some numbers to front line fighter *Gruppen* and did at least give pilots a chance to score a kill or two beyond the range of the bombers' defensive fire. However, the cumbersome and unguided weapons were merely spin-stabilised, time-fused adaptations of the standard Wgr 21 *Nebelwerfer* infantry rocket. Powerful though they were, being limited to only two shots per sortie hardly gave the pilots who used them any great confidence in the weapon.

Bombs

Included in the Bf 109's original design was an internal bomb cell, the So-3. Containing five 22 lb (10-kg) bombs, the cell was an ingenious attempt to provide the fighter with additional offensive capability without resort to drag-inducing external carriers. Located immediately aft of the pilot's seat and close to the aircraft's centre of gravity, the So-3 was abandoned soon after the prototype flew.

During the production run of the early model Bf 109s a series of streamlined ETC centreline racks were designed to act as carriers for bombs or a single drop tank. These could be used operationally by all models but were first fitted extensively on the Bf 109E.

Using adaptations of the standard Revi gunsight to aim their weapons, the Bf 109Es of any *Jagdbomber* unit could carry a range of ordnance. A single 550 lb (SC 250 kg) bomb was most commonly carried on an ETC 500/IXb centreline belly rack. Four 110 lb (50 kg) SC 50 bombs could be carried on the ETC 50/VIIId rack, which was recessed to provide adequate ground clearance for the bomb fins on take off. A multiple dispenser for 96 SD-2 anti-personnel bombs carried by the Bf 109E-4/B in the early stages of Operation *Barbarossa* does not appear to have seen widespread use elsewhere.

Due to stress considerations, the Bf 109 was not adapted to carry bombs under the wings, but reconnaissance models were fitted with suitable racks to take a pair of drop tanks outboard of the undercarriage wells.

The Bf 109's bomb rack could carry a standard 66-gal (300 litre) drop tank. One of the many questions surrounding Luftwaffe strategy is why tanks were not used much earlier to extend the range of the Bf 109.

Fuel Tanks

While not using drop tanks as much as the Allies, the Germans often needed to boost the range of the Bf 109. The 66-Imp gal (300 litre) Junkers/NKF centreline tank was used in all theatres. Early tanks were of a wood composite construction. They were quite prone to leakage, causing some prejudice against them although improvements were made and late-war external tanks were reliable enough.

There is some evidence to suggest that any reluctance by individual pilots to carry a drop tank stemmed from the fact that they could not always be jettisoned as fast as was desirable. Gun camera film of Bf 109s (and Fw 190s) under attack by Allied aircraft shows pilots retaining their external tanks in combat, occasionally with disastrous consequences if they were struck directly by machine gun or cannon rounds. This may have been due to inexperience, though it remains a matter of conjecture whether jettisoning them could be difficult, particularly under high G loadings.

Postwar armament

The Avia S.199 perpetuated the armament layout of the Bf 109, but with the centreline cannon deleted in favour of two 20-mm wing cannon and two cowl-mounted 7.9-mm machine guns.

Wing guns for the Spanish Hispano HA-1112s were CETME 12.7-mm calibre machine guns or 20-mm HS-404 cannon. Oerlikon 10 kg air-to-ground rockets were carried by the final production versions of the *Buchon*.

Appendix 2
Technical Specifications

Bf 109 V1
Type: single-seat fighter
Powerplant: 583 hp Rolls-Royce Kestrel II S
Dimensions:
span   32 ft 4.5 in (9.87 m)
length   28 ft 5 in (8.70 m)
height   8 ft 2in (2.50 m)
wing area   172.16 ft² (16 m²)
Weights:
empty   3,307 lb (1 500 kg)
loaded   3,970 lb (1 800 kg)
wing loading   134.5 lb/ft² (125 kg/m²)*
Performance:
maximum speed   292 mph (470 km/h)
cruising speed   217 mph (350 km/h)
service ceiling   26,900 ft (8 200 m)
range   435 miles (700 km)
Armament: none
* Note: This figure is based on the Bf 109B, and was almost certainly lower in reality

Bf 109B-1
Type: single-seat fighter
Powerplant: 680 hp Jumo 210 D
Dimensions:
span   32 ft 4.5 in (9.87 m)
length   28 ft 5 in (8.70 m)
height   8 ft 2 in (2.5 m)
wing area   175.92 ft² (16.35 m²)
Weights:
empty   3,483 lb (1 580 kg)
loaded   4,520 lb (2 050 kg)
wing loading   134.5 lb/ft² (125 kg/m²)
Performance:
maximum speed   302 mph (486 km/h)
cruising speed   217 mph (350 km/h)
service ceiling   29,520 ft (8 997 m)
range   279 miles (450 km)
Armament: 2 or 3 x MG 17 machine guns

Bf 109E-3
Type: single-seat fighter/bomber
Powerplant: 1,100 hp DB 601 A
Dimensions:
span   32 ft 4.5 in (9.87 m)
length   28 ft 4.50 in (8.66 m)
height   8 ft 2 in (2.5 m)
wing area   174.05 ft² (16.35 m²)
Weights:
empty   4, 685 lb (2,125 kg)

loaded   5,875 lb (2,665 kg)
wing loading   140.9 lb/ft² (131 kg/m²)
Performance:
maximum speed   345 mph (555 km/h)
cruising speed   300 mph (483 km/h)
service ceiling   33,760 ft (10 290 m)
range   410 miles (660 km)
Armament: 2 x MG 17 machine guns;
2 x MG FF cannon

Bf 109G-6
Type: single-seat fighter/bomber
Powerplant: 1,475 hp DB 605 A
Dimensions:
span   32 ft 6.5 in (9.92 m)
length   29 ft 0.25 in (8.94 m)
height   8 ft 2.5 in (2.51 m)
wing area   173.3 ft² (16.02 m²)
Weights:
empty   5,893 lb (2,680 kg)
loaded   6,940 lb (3,200 kg)
wing loading   180.7 lb/ft² (168 kg m²)
Performance:
maximum speed   386 mph (621 km/h)
cruising speed   323 mph (520 km/h)
service ceiling   37,890 ft (11 550 m)
range   359 miles (563 km)
Armament: 2 x MG 131 machine guns
1 x MG 151/20 cannon

Bf 109K-4
Type: single-seat fighter
Powerplant: 1,800 hp DB 605 D
Dimensions:
span   32 ft 6.5 in (9.92 m)
length   29 ft 0.25 in (9.02 m)
height   8 ft 2.5 in (2.50 m)
wing area   173.3 ft² (16.5 m²)
Weights:
empty   6,074 lb (2 755 kg)
loaded   7,438 lb (3 400 kg)
wing loading   178 lb/ft² (168 kg/m²)
Performance:
maximum speed   452 mph (728 km/h)
cruising speed   401 mph (645 km/h)
service ceiling   41,012 ft (12 500 m)
range   401 miles (645 km)
Armament: 2 x MG 131 or 151 machine guns
1 x MK 108 cannon

Appendix 3
Bf 109 Production

Series production of the Bf 109 was initiated at BFW's main plant at **Augsburg**, and from March 1937 at a new facility at **Regensburg**. Together they produced 10,888 examples, approximately a third of all aircraft built. BFW became Messerschmitt AG on 11 July 1938 and thereafter adopted the abbreviation 'Me' for new aircraft, although the original abbreviation for *'Bayerische Flugwerke'* was generally retained for the Bf 109. Messerschmitt ultimately became the largest aircraft manufacturer in Germany during WWII.

Additional Bf 109 production lines were established at **Wiener Neustadt** (WNF) in Austria and **WNF Leipzig**, and by licensing agreements with **Fiesele**r at Kassel, **Focke-Wulf** at Bremen and **Erla-Machinenwerk**, an industrial construction and repair complex that eventually controlled several main plants including Erla VII at Antwerp in Belgium. Erla built more Bf 109s than any other sub-contractor, about 32 per cent. Other aircraft manufacturers brought into the Bf 109 programme included **Ago** at Oschersleben and **Arado** at Warnemunde.

Annual production figures for Bf 109s are contradictory and incomplete but among those quoted are totals of approximately 2,634 in 1941 and 2,664 in 1942, a total of 5,298 Bf 109Fs and Gs. Figures for production lost in Allied air raids are equally incomplete but there are indicators; for Messerschmitt these began with the 8th Air Force attack of 17 August 1943. Earlier in 1943, Erla at Antwerp had been bombed on 5 April and Fieseler at Kassel on 28 July. Wiener Neustadt was hit on 14 August, cutting the Bf 109 output of 270 for July to 184 in August. The 8th AAF was back over Regensburg in October to round out a difficult year for Messerschmitt – yet in spite of the raids Bf 109 production had actually risen, to 6,279 for 1943. Part of the total was made up by 93 completed examples (out of 900 ordered) from Hungarian and Bulgarian sub-contractors.

The rising intensity of Allied air raids meant that things could only get worse. Early in 1944 the USAAF and RAF Bomber Command launched their 'Big Week' series of raids on the German aircraft industry. The result was the loss of 350 Bf 109s at WNF Leipzig, 150 at Augsburg and Regensburg and 200 at WNF, a total of 700 aircraft. All fighter assembly plants were firmly on USAAF and RAF target lists and would remain so until production at some plants was brought virtually to a standstill.

During 1944 Albert Speer's armaments ministry instituted a series of radical measures to concentrate German aircraft manufacture almost totally on fighter production, at the same time reducing vulnerability to attack by utilising several hundred plants. In this way a third source of Bf 109s emerged in addition to the home-based plants and those in foreign countries . Speer set up a network of dispersed sites all over Germany, factories being established in any convenient area that was secure from bomb damage, including railway tunnels and disused mines.

These plants often took time to become as productive as planned, and some never came on stream. The quality of workmanship varied depending on the source of labour – it is a fact that the build quality of some aircraft produced in Germany, including the Bf 109, fell markedly compared to those completed by the skilled workforce in Hungary. The industry had to fight to keep skilled assembly line workers, who were constantly being called up for combat service by the armed forces.

To supplement the output from the main sub-contractors BFW/Messerschmitt issued licences for the Bf 109 to be produced in Hungary (**Gyor Wagonfabrik**) Rumania (**I.A.R**) and Czechoslovakia (**Avia**). The number of deliveries from these sources varied – as indeed does the total number of Bf 109s built. However, the figure of 33,675 seems to have become accepted as correct.

Appendix 4
Main Production Variants

Several hundred Bf 109s were completed before the advent of the Bf109E, the first major production variant. The early machines included 30 or more *Versuchs* or prototype aircraft, most of which were either retained and owned by BFW or 'leased back' from the RLM, as required. Some confusion remains over the designation 'Bf 109A' which although being the logical suffix letter to start off production, rarely seems to have been mentioned in documentation. It may well have been retrospectively applied to these first examples and has been used as such in this book. This table lists each production variant of the Bf 109, together with a note on the constructor and the number built, where known.

Note: Mtt R - Messerschmitt Regensburg
      Mtt A - Messerschmitt Augsburg

Prototypes
31 (approx)

Bf 109A
20 including the V3 and V10 (possibly two other examples)

Bf 109B-1:
341 built by BFW, Erla and Fieseler; sole production variant

Bf 109C-1:
58 completed at Augsburg

Bf 109D-1
647 built by Ago, Arado, Erla, Fieseler and Focke-Wulf; also Mtt R

Bf 109E
Bf 109E-0
    10 initial examples completed by Mtt R plus 10 at other plants
Bf 109E-1 and E-1/B
    1,183 completed at Mtt A, FW, Ago, Fi and Ar.W
Bf 109E-3
    1,171 at Mtt A and Mtt R, Erla and WNF
Bf 109E-3a
    1,321 Export version built at Mtt R
Bf 109E-3/B
    Conversions; fighter-bomber variant order for 500 aircraft apparently initiated by the RLM on 11 June 1940

Bf 109E-4
    250 built at Mtt R, Erla and WNF
Bf 109E-4/B
    211 at Mtt R, Erla and WNF
Bf 109E-4/BN
    35 at Mtt R and WNF (total E-4 = 496)
Bf 109E-5
    29 built by Ar.W
Bf 109E-6/N
    9 built by Ar.W
Bf 109E-7/N
    452 at Mtt R; Erla, Fi, Ar.W and WNF
Bf 109E-7/NZ
    Some built within E-7/N batches
Bf 109E-8
    60 by Fi and Ar. W
Bf 109E-9
    Small number of reconnaisance model conversions

Bf 109T
Bf 109T-1
    7 aircraft; out of sequence designation applied to experimental carrier conversions based on the Bf 109 E-3;
Bf 109T-2
    70 aircraft; out of sequence designation applied to land-based 'denavalised' carrier conversions (surviving examples of the original 70 aircraft) with DB 601 N engine

Bf 109F
Bf 109F-0
    11 built by Mtt R in 1940; plus 23 in 1941
Bf 109F-1
    208 built (49 by WNF and 157 by Mtt R)
Bf 109F-2
    1,380 (approx)
Bf 109F-3
    50 built
Bf 109F-4
    1,841 built by WNF and Erla
Bf 109F-5
    1 only built by WNF

Bf 109G
Bf 109G-0
    11 built
Bf 109G-1
    167 built by WNF and Mtt R
Bf 109G-2
    1,586 - Erla, WNF and Mtt R plus one by Gyor as Ga-2

Bf 109G-3
    50 - Mtt R
Bf 109G-4
    1,242 (approx) - Erla, WNF, Mtt R and three by Gyor as Ga-4
Bf 109G-5
    16 (approx) plus conversions by Erla
Bf 109G-6
    12,000 (approx) - Erla, WNF, Mtt R and Gyor
    NB: This figure seems an over estimate as it puts the total number of all aircraft built way over 33,000; the author would put it at slightly less than 10,000
Bf 109G-8
    906 - 167 by WNF; plus 739 G-8/R5
Bf 109G-10
    2,600 (approx)
Bf 109G-12
    Conversions only 500 (approx) two seat trainers from existing G-series airframes
Bf 109G-14
    5,500 (approx) - Erla, WNF and Mtt R
Bf 109G-14/AS
    1,000 (approx)

Bf 109K
Bf 109K-2
    1 only - Mtt R
Bf 109K-4
    1,693 built by Mtt R
Bf 109K-6
    1 only?

Note:
It is apparent that the Messerschmitt plants produced many more times the number of components than were needed to complete a given production run of the Bf 109, particularly tailplane sections. That is quite understandable considering the fluctuating figures for orders and is surely the reason that numerous late war Bf 109G-14s were fitted not with the specified taller tail surfaces but the original fin and rudder. A cutback in the manufacture of spare components resulting from a materials shortage would inevitably bring about a run on existing stocks. After the surrender Allied troops found warehouses, train wagons, trucks and so forth filled with new Bf 109 parts and these stocks, while they lasted, would logically have been used to complete new airframes.

Appendix 5
Museum Aircraft and Survivors

Only long after the Allies had finally completed the destruction of the *Luftwaffe* and thousands of Bf 109s along with all other German aircraft had been bulldozed, burned or hacked into saucepan-size pieces, did someone give thought to preserving one or two examples. There were precious few survivors from the giant production machine that Messerschmitt AG had become during the war, but the preservation process began almost accidentally with those early Bf 109Es that had been captured and evaluated by the Allies. Some of these were shipped abroad to give American and Commonwealth pilots a chance to see exactly what they might soon be up against, and of these survivors, at least 12 were given permanent homes in museums as far apart as South Africa and Yugoslavia. Most of these museums kept their early Bf 109 acquisitions and since the war the current world wide figure of original Bf 109s on display, in storage or under restoration has risen to 34.*

Original Bf 109s, particularly of the later G series, remain rare however. Of the above total only two are listed as G-10s and three as G-14s, there being no example of the Bf 109K. Several G-6s are currently under 'rebuild to fly' status or are subject to full restoration as ground exhibits. The opening up of the former Soviet Union has meant that survivors of the huge air war on the Eastern Front are being unearthed – sometimes literally – in remote corners of a vast, often inhospitable terrain. Fully realising the value that a rebuilt Bf 109 can fetch on today's warbird market, recovery teams have an abiding interest in finding such relics. Among the virtually complete Bf 109s found in Russia is an F-4 (WNr 10132), in the UK for restoration at time of writing.

With the almost total demise of the Avia S.199s after passing from Czech and Israeli service, it was extremely fortuitous for the modern warbird scene that the postwar Spanish Air Force opted to extend the life of its Bf 109E airframes. By installing a 1,600 hp Rolls-Royce Merlin 500 engine driving a four-blade airscrew, the aircraft became a CASA Ca-1112. Series production finally centred on the HA-1112-M1L, the C-4-K in the *Ejercito del Aire*. Serving from 1955 until 1965, the *Buchons* were declared surplus and put up for sale in 1967 – just in time to appear as 'Bf 109Es' in the film 'Battle of Britain' Most of the

28 *Buchons* purchased were sold on, and have been seen around the world in various paint schemes representing wartime Bf 109Es, Fs and Gs. The engine cowling contours of the Merlin, which, unlike the original Daimler-Benz powerplant, was a conventional V-12, made the Ca-1112's origins hard to disguise, but as the nearest clone of a genuine Bf 109, the chance to own and/or fly this hybrid was rarely passed up. Today 30 HA-1112 M1Ls and K1Ls which are airworthy, under restoration or on display swell the list of Bf 109 derivatives. Finally, three Avias (all listed as CS 199s) are extant in the Czech Republic (two) and Israel (one).

The real thing remained so scarce that for years few expected to see a Bf 109 fly again. But provided an example was available, there was no real reason why a wartime Bf 109 could not take to the air once more. Flt Lt Russ Snadden accepted that challenge in September 1972. He took the RAF's Bf 109G-2/trop (WNr 10639) into care and finally achieved a personal goal of seeing it take to the air again on 17 March 1991. It was 49 years, 19 of which had been spent in restoration, since it had been abandoned by 8./JG 77 in the desert during October 1942. Sadly, after six years on the air show circuit 'Black 6' crashed on 12 October 1997 and suffered extensive damage, enough to make its re-restoration to airworthiness a doomed prospect although it has been repaired to static exhibit standard.

An alternative to retaining the Merlin in a Spanish airframe is to install a DB 601. That was done for the HA-1112 owned by Messerschmitt-Bolkow-Blohm, now the Messerschmitt Foundation, which apparently did not find the marriage as happy as might be supposed. Having crash-landed at least three times, the aircraft flies under Bf 109G guise, German registered as D-FMBB and fuselage coded FM+BB in the style of a *Stammkirchen*.

Other genuine Bf 109s are meanwhile being made flyable in the UK, the US and Germany, where dedicated bands of enthusiasts and engineers work hard to create what is a major air show attraction almost anywhere in the world.

* Believed correct as of January 2002

Appendix 6
Bf 109 Kits and Accessories

Among the world's most popular model subjects, the Messerschmitt Bf 109 has been included in the ranges of all the leading manufacturers since kits moulded in polystyrene plastic became generally available during the late 1950s. Both the flagship injection-moulded companies and specialist 'short run' suppliers, working first with vacuform plastic and latterly with resin, have offered kits and enough alternative parts to enable the skilled modeller to complete the entire Messerschmitt Bf 109 range.

Among the earliest Bf 109 kits in the ever-popular 1/72nd scale was that from **Airfix** of the UK, while the American concerns **Aurora** and **Monogram** were early entrants in the 1/48th scale field. Few of these 'pioneer' kits would win any prizes for accuracy today, but in the intervening decades, Bf 109 kits appeared regularly, with toolmakers showing greater awareness of the subtle contours of the full size aircraft and designing their models accordingly. The improving standards resulted in superb 1/48th replicas, particularly from **Revell**, **Fujimi**, **Hasegawa** and **HobbyCraft**.

Most manufacturers with a 1/72nd scale range included the '109, but generally with less accuracy than was achieved with the larger kits. A degree of conversion work and some cross kitting was invariably needed whatever the variant chosen – but just as this book was completed **Tamiya** released a Bf 109E-4. First reports indicate that this appears to be one of the best kits of the Bf 109 in any scale. It seems as though modellers wanting a kit that lends itself to hundreds of colour schemes can at last be built 'straight from the box' – after waiting for about 50 years!

While the kit producers have tended to opt first for Emils, then for the very popular late-war Bf 109Gs and Ks, the very early versions of the aircraft were generally overlooked entirely. But in the last decade or so they have finally appeared with **HobbyCraft** taking a lead. The company's 1/48th injection-moulded kits of the Bf 109B, C and D as well as early and late production Bf 109Es, are good representations of their subjects.

Further up the scale ladder to 1/32nd, there has been a Bf 109F/G from **Revell** and Emils from **Matchbox** and **Hasegawa**. The latter is an excellent kit, well up to this manufacturer's high standards. In the 1970s **Airfix** added a Bf 109E to their 1/24th scale range, complete with a companion 'guide book' on how to super-detail the basic kit, incorporate the model into dioramas utilising the pilot figure supplied and suggested undertaking conversion to the Jumo engined Bf 109B and D.

Messerschmitt's design habit of having most of the engine, ammunition storage and other areas accessible via hinged panels is of benefit to the modeller. He may show most of the innards of the aircraft with the panels still attached rather than (as with some Allied types) to have to resort to a diorama-type display of dislocated panels which were invarably removed during servicing.

The parallel increase in better Bf 109 kits and reference literature spurred wider knowledge of different paint finishes and markings, particularly those flown by the numerous *Experten*. This led a number of specialist decal sheet suppliers to regularly add Bf 109 subjects in various scales to their lists. Companies such as **AeroMaster**, **Cutting Edge** and **Third Group** continue to offer high-quality sheets covering the markings of the famous and less well known Messerschmitt pilots.

A new release in 1/32nd scale is the **Revell** Bf 109G – an excellent and useful kit with endless possibilities for marking and detailing.

Appendix 7
Bf 109 Books

Although the Bf 109 has been the subject of hundreds of books, the serious reader who requires accurate information is advised to concentrate on the most recently-published volumes. It seems that the more recent the book, the more accurate the information is likely to be, because new information on the *Luftwaffe* is constantly coming to light. Operational unit histories, particularly those by Jochen Prien which have concentrated thus far on Bf 109 units, have also proliferated in recent years and are a fascinating source of study.

Carson, L: Pursue & Destroy;
Sentry Books, Grenada Hills, California, 1978

Griel, Manfred: Messerschmitt Bf 109G/K (The Luftwaffe Profile Series No 2);
Schiffer Publishing Ltd, Atglen, PA, 1995

Hooton, E R: Phoenix Triumphant: The Rise and Rise of the Luftwaffe;
Arms and Armour, London 1994

Hooton, E R: Eagle in Flames: The Fall of the Luftwaffe;
Arms and Armour, London, 1997

Janda, Ales & Poruba, Tomas: Messerschmitt Bf 109K;
JaPo, Hradek Kralove, Czech Republic, 1997

Mermet, Jean-Claude: Messerschmitt Bf 109 G-1 through K-4 - Engines and fittings;
J-C Mermet, France, 1999

Mombeek, Eric: Defenders of the Reich; JG 1 Vol one 1939-42;
Classic Publications, Crowborough, E Sussex, 2001

Mombeek, Eric: Defending the Reich: history of JG 1 'Oesau';
JAC Publications, Norwich, Norfolk, 1992

Poruba, Tomas & Mol, Kees: Messerschmitt Bf 109K camouflage and markings;
JaPo, Hradec Kralove, Czech Republic, 2000

Radinger, Willy & Schick, Walter: Messerschmitt Bf 109 A - E;
Schiffer, Atglen, PA, 1999

Reis, Karl & Ring, Hans: The Legion Condor;
Schiffer, Atglen, PA, 1992

Schmoll, Peter: Die Messerschmitt-Werke im Zweiten Weltkreig;
Mittelbayerische Druck-und Verlags-Gesellschaft mbH, Regensburg, 1998

Scutts, Jerry: Messerschmitt Bf 109 Aces of North Africa and the Mediterranean; (Osprey Aircraft of the Aces 2);
Reed Consumer Books Ltd, London,1994

Scutts, Jerry: Messerschmitt Bf 109 The Operational Record;
Airlife Publishing, Shrewsbury, 1996

Weal, John: Bf 109D/E Aces 1939-41 (Osprey Aircraft of the Aces 11);
Reed Consumer Books Ltd, London, 1996

Weal, John: Bf 109F/G/K Aces of the Western Front (Osprey Aircraft of the Aces 29);
Osprey Publishing Ltd, Botley, Oxford, 1999

Weal, John: Bf 109 Aces of the Russian Front (Osprey Aircraft of the Aces 37);
Osprey Publishing Ltd, Botley, Oxford, 2001

Weal, John: Jagdgeschwader 2 'Richthofen' (Osprey Aviation Elite 1);
Osprey Publishing Ltd, Botley, Oxford, 2001

Williams, Anthony G: Rapid Fire;
Airlife Publishing, Shrewsbury, 2000

Index